The Inner-City of God

John Pridmore was Rector of Hackney in London's East End until his recent retirement. Previously he was on the staff of St Martin-in-the-Fields. His earlier career was in teaching and chaplaincy, at Ridley Hall, Cambridge, and in schools in England and Africa. He is a regular columnist in the *Church Times*. He lives in Brighton.

The Inner-City of God

The diary of an East End parson

John Pridmore

CANTERBURY
PRESS
Norwich

© John Pridmore 2008

First published in 2008 by the Canterbury Press Norwich
(a publishing imprint of Hymns Ancient & Modern Limited,
a registered charity)
13–17 Long Lane, London EC1A 9PN

www.scm-canterburypress.co.uk

British Library Cataloguing in Publication data

A catalogue record for this book is available
from the British Library

ISBN 978-1-85311-882-1

Typeset by Regent Typesetting, London
Printed in the UK by
CPI William Clowes Beccles NR34 7TL

For my family and friends

Contents

Foreword

This book made me laugh out loud, but it also made me cry. It is about what it means to be faithful to Christ even if you are not successful, which is how life is for most of us even though we want both. So you might want to put this book down now before it does anything to you.

Like John Pridmore, I was an East-End parish priest. Our journeys went in opposite directions. In the summer of 1995 I moved west with my family from the Isle of Dogs in Tower Hamlets to St Martin-in-the-Fields in Trafalgar Square, and John moved east with his from St Martin's to be the Rector of Hackney. I had known several of his Hackney predecessors. It is not an easy job. These pages testify how close it came to breaking him.

I grew up in safe suburban north London. I do not despise my roots and am grateful for nearly everything, but by the age of eighteen I was longing to break free. Now what hope I have for the Church of England belongs almost entirely to those places, rural and urban, where the conventional has pretty much broken down. It is the prerequisite for resurrection, for being broken open.

On the Isle of Dogs in the late 1980s, after there had been a great deal of tension in urban priority areas across the country and the Church of England had responded with the Archbishop's Commission 'Faith in the City', we received visits from a succession of government ministers. They each said that the Conservatives did not have a footing in areas like ours and didn't know or understand them. These ministers belonged to the church and had the wit to ask the local church to help interpret and explain. In these meetings we talked from our experience, and the ministers got cross and told us we were wrong. They left with no greater understanding and we were left with even less respect for those who governed us.

If you don't live in Hackney or one of the many deprived inner urban communities, or if you do and your experience of these very varied places is different to that described in this book, look carefully at what John Pridmore writes that makes you angry, because that is where you will find your greatest learning. This book is based on his diary, sections of which have been published over the years in the *Church Times*. It is immediate, raw, good-humoured and sometimes very painful. So much of it had to be endured and was beyond control.

Having been part of the team that has just renewed the buildings of St Martin-in-the-Fields more or less successfully, I found the story of the impossible 2,000 seat St John-at-Hackney particularly depressing. Yet how many churches struggle to make contemporary sense of their heritage and how delightful is the story in the following chapter, on the Jerusalem Space created in what had been a small toilet in the local secondary school with its Mark Cazalet triptych, 'Christ the Light of Hackney'. It was on a scale that could be coped with.

Thirty years ago, when training for ordination, a cartoonist who is also a priest gave me three cartoons of clerical life. One is of a young curate trying on the bishop's mitre while the old man slept in an armchair in the room next door. The second is of a middle-aged vicar manically competing in the sack race at the Church Fete, expending incredible energy and grinning at all and sundry. The third is of an old and gentle man with a broad-rimmed clerical hat cycling serenely over a tack which will burst his tyre and his serenity.

The erstwhile Rector of Hackney is not serene. He saw through himself a long time ago. It would be easy to mistake his diary for cynicism but it is much more like the Wisdom literature of the

Scriptures. Knowing himself, he proclaims a gospel of grace, free but by no means cheap. He never had a vocation to run an organization, something which won't have endeared him to the modern Church of England wanting to become a more coherent and managed organization because we are so anxious about numbers and our own survival. Yet I will not be the only more assiduously managerial parish priest with a deep admiration for his ministry.

A long time ago, I used to teach a course on mission to students training for ordination. Nowadays everything in the Church of England is alleged to be mission, but this was one of the first courses of its kind. The lesson I hope my students learned, that has certainly not been learned by the church at large, is the simple one that people join churches which are worth joining. Dumbing down, or evading reality, are not good options in the long run.

In *The Inner-City of God* there is the experience of a priest mediating between God and people in difficult circumstances. It is intelligent, provocative, gracious and intensely moving. You can feel the spiritual strain in these pages, fingering as it so often does the problems of the inner-city and the contemporary Church of England through the local and particular. In Hackney, salvation is to be found in 'the trivial transfigured'. In a different time and place this is what another Church of England parish priest, the poet George Herbert, called 'God in ordinary'; and it is anything but.

The Revd Nicholas Holtam
Vicar, St Martin-in-the-Fields

1

Introduction

Today someone set fire to the contents of the council skip permanently parked at the corner of our churchyard. A small boy is standing on the churchyard wall, peeing into the conflagration. Why do I suddenly wonder whether I'm doing any good?

For eleven years I was Rector of Hackney, for some the worst place in Britain to live. During those years I kept a diary and the above cameo is an extract from it. This book is largely a collage of such cuttings, thumb-nail sketches of the life of one inner-city parson who tried, rarely successfully, to cope with the twin demands of an inner-city parish and the exasperating organization he worked for, the Church of England.

My hope is that these snapshots might say something of more than local interest, that they might offer a fresh perspective on the mission and ministry of a church profoundly confused about what it is here for. Often something would happen and I would wonder what it meant. That curiosity accounts for the commentary on the cameos I have cherry-picked from my diary. There is the faintest whiff of theology in these pages. The theology attempted, such as it is, is of a particular kind. It is theology shaped by what happens, by when it happens, and by where it happens. It is inner-city theology, street-theology. It's hammered out in – and by – Hackney. Like Hackney, it's messy.

Theology shaped by events and places is sometimes called 'contextual theology'. The context may be as momentous as the Fall of Jerusalem or as trivial as a boy relieving himself in a burning skip. The theological work starts when we ask what, here and now, is being said to us. In reality theology is always contextual. The context of academic theology is typically a library or a book-lined study, somewhere undistracted by what is going on. Of course some things are best done in such places. The bus queue is not an ideal place in which to master New Testament Greek, especially if you are waiting for a bus in Hackney. But theology was not born in a library, any more than Jesus was, nor is it where it thrives. The vibrant theology of the Bible, so far from being uninstructed by what was going on, was *determined* by what was going on. That principle, that what matters theologically emerges from experience, guides what went into my diary and what goes into this book. In a word, Hackney made me think again about what it means to be a Christian.

One simple question dogged me like a bad tooth while I was in Hackney: 'What would we do in this situation if, just for a moment, we assumed that Christianity was true?' For the sake of their sanity, it is a question that Church of England incumbents should probably never ask. But – whether it was conscience or cussedness goading me, I do not know – I found that I could not ignore it. I realized that in my job I was regularly being asked to obey imperatives very far from those of the Christian gospel. If I harp over-much on some matters – the church's enslavement to its buildings, its continuing marginalization of children, its paralysing bureaucracy, for example – I can only plead that that is what toothache does to you.

Mine was not a daily diary. A parish priest's life can be richly rewarding, but much of it these days is boring, far too tedious to record. The monotony of their days follows from the fact that clergy are increasingly required to work as managers rather than ministers. One image of the church in the New Testament is that of a caravan of nomads, a company that travels light and never settles for long in one place, a fellowship of 'strangers and pilgrims on the earth'. That image does not describe the contemporary Church of England. The church of my baptism is now more like a business with branches. Incumbents are the local managers. We have more in common with Boots than the Bedouin. Much of the time minding the shop is rather dull.

Sometimes it seems to me that there have been three periods in Christian history. First came the prophet, notably that eccentric itinerant exorcist known as Jesus bar-Joseph. There followed the age of the priest, a dispensation lasting until quite recently. Now there has dawned a darker chapter, that of the planner. The ascendancy of the management culture in the church mirrors what is happening in many other institutions, notoriously in education and in the health service. Professor Richard Roberts of Lancaster University argues that we are witnessing in the contemporary Church of England the 'consolidation of top-down efficacy and efficiency . . . the triumph of a managerial performance culture, concerned with religious product delivery'.[1]

It is all deeply depressing. Or it would be if it were the whole story. The life of the church is organic and its powerful inner springs cannot be contained within the channels prescribed for it. The common life of the church and the daily life of a parish priest are occasionally 'brushed by transcendence', blessed by moments when the veil between this world and a better one seems very thin. Such times, as fleeting as they are eternally significant, escape all the matrices and grids within which the centralizing bureaucracy of the modern church seeks to accommodate and control the parson's life. All the most memorable and rewarding experiences of my life as an inner-city clergyman have been unplanned.

These are the experiences on which I reflect in this diary. I offer a montage of the absurd, the poignant, and the occasionally glorious. These jottings are not a record of 'good practice', nor do they illustrate better ways of 'being church', nor are there here any 'fresh expressions of church'. (Having got those grisly gobbets of vulgar jargon off my chest I feel better. I shall try not to repeat them.) My diary is simply a sequence of scenes from the divine comedy played out in one inner-city parish. I have tried, though not very hard, to arrange them in some sort of order. That order is not chronological. I do not subscribe to the myth of progress and I am far from sure that in my eleven years in Hackney

I got anywhere. The arrangement, such as it is, is thematic.

My diary is not just about Hackney. There are memories of what went before. Sometimes people ask me, 'What took you to Hackney?' The answer is a winding and wayward path. 'God does not send his rivers like arrows to the sea,' said John Oman. I shall briefly sketch some of the twists and turns of the river that bore me to Hackney, my pilgrim's progress to the inner-city of God.

As I reread my diary I notice just how many memories crowd its pages. I hope that this tendency to look back is not the kind of crippling nostalgia that forbids engagement with the immediate. Most of the reminiscences in my diary are prompted by gratitude. As I muddled through on a whinge and a prayer, mentors from long ago whispered in my ear. I survived in the inner-city, if I did, because shards of their wisdom were still lodged in my memory. Occasionally I shall get out of the way to allow their voices to be heard.

And then to love Hackney you must sometimes leave it. I was grateful for a 'sabbatical' half-way through my Hackney years. (Nowadays our hyper-active church insists that such breaks are not 'sabbaticals', but 'study-leaves'.) As a family we took our full complement of holidays and, some years, a day or two more. There are clergy in the East End who rarely take time off. Some I suspect rarely go to bed. I am not persuaded that their churches profit from such relentless solicitude and dedication to duty. Certainly it was not my style. (Nor was it the style of one of our local clergy during my time in Cornwall, the Rector of St Crewenna's, Praze-an-Beeble. This dear man spent much of the week sitting quietly on a cliff-top observing the last surviving Cornish chough. I no longer despise him quite as much as I once did.) I believe that I understood Hackney better, and perhaps was of more use in the place, by sometimes being somewhere else. The days and weeks off and that one sabbatical were not, I hope, solely self-indulgence.

My family – my wife Pat, my daughter Rebecca (not to speak of our various animals) – features in these pages. Parish life was a roller-coaster that we rode together. It was my family who again and again saved me from the bottle or the attention of men in long white coats. The essential boundaries between family life and parish life are exceedingly difficult to maintain, as every priest, besieged in a rectory or vicarage beside their church, will testify. Fortunately it has not been necessary to maintain those boundaries within this book.

There were other outings too. The church year is a cycle of saints days and holy seasons. It is also a calendar of conferences. Clergy, though they will deny it, love conferences and they organize and attend an awful lot of them. Bishops adore conferences and regularly summon their clergy to them. Few conferences do any good. Last year's conference is as swiftly forgotten as last Sunday's sermon. But they get you out of the parish for a few days and these pages are evidence that I was not man enough altogether to renounce them.

Diaries are personal documents reflecting personal predilections and prejudices. To say that is to try to excuse the prominence of books in these entries, though I have mostly confined my notes on them to one chapter. I belong to a generation of clergy now passing which was taught that one's morning should be spent in one's study – and certainly not answering bumph in brown envelopes or its electronic equivalent. I believe in that pattern as an ideal, although I found it hard to achieve. I am not ashamed that I sometimes chose to read and write rather than to be out and about. And I make no apology for always having preferred an interesting and important book to a boring and futile meeting. At my farewell do a friend was kind enough to suggest that I was well-read. If there is any truth in that tribute, it partly reflects my poor attendance at Deanery Synod.

Much here savours of your own correspondent's report from the land where the Bong tree grows. Often in the course of my duties as a clergyman, when required to do something utterly idiotic, I found myself asking with Wilfred Owen, 'Was it for this that the clay grew tall?' But, thank God, the trivial can sometimes be transfigured. For Julian of Norwich, the hazel-nut she found in the corner of her cell was a demonstration of the love of God. Some say much the same about the mass-produced wafer handed to them at an altar rail.

2

Pilgrim's Progress

I wake to the smell of smoke. It is not the Rectory which is burning. Nor, alas, is it the Last Fire, the final conflagration in which all our sins and follies will be consumed. It's Gibbons that's in flames. Gibbons, just over the road from us, is – or was – Hackney's one department store. It was built over a century ago and to all appearances neither its stock nor its staff had been replaced since then. I never saw a customer go into Gibbons. The place was run by two or three ancients, melancholy figures in grubby blue overalls who stood all day at the door of the store, sucking their cigarettes, nursing their secret sorrows. I hurry over to the inferno. Scores of firemen are fighting the flames. Ambulance crews are standing by. The police are keeping the ghouls at a distance. Even the Salvation Army is there, with their mobile canteen, dispensing mugs of tea and bacon butties. Everyone has a role, a task to perform. Apart, that is, from this absurd vicar with his studiously composed expression of benevolence and distress. I ask a policeman whether there is anything I can do. Apparently not. Not for the first time, I wonder what I'm here for.

I was born in suburbia, that neither-here-nor-there region 'halfway between the shops and the fields' as James Kenward called it. I grew up in the Second World War, an only child and a lonely child. Our semi-detached house in Sidcup was in bomb-alley. My first prayer, as I recall, was to ask God to make the 'doodlebug', whose engine I heard guttering to a halt above us, fall on someone else's house. I went to an awful prep school where I was bullied and intermittently beaten – I rarely knew why – and where I learned 'amo, amas, amat'. My secondary school was Dulwich College, a 'direct-grant' school in those post-war years. We were all scholarship boys, so my parents didn't pay a penny. Dulwich was a good school for you if you were sporty or bright. The rest of us suffered what my dentist once said he saw in my teeth, 'controlled neglect'. The Headmaster ('The Master', as the head at Dulwich is always known) was Christopher Gilkes. In my days at Dulwich he said only six words to me – 'Bend over' three times. The school had an unheated open-air swimming pool in which we were made to swim once a week with nothing on. I have not returned to Dulwich recently so I do not know whether bathing in the buff is still compulsory. I owe an incalculable debt to one of my teachers, 'Doggy' Marriot, who in the holidays bowled unplayable leg-spinners for Kent and England and who in term time introduced me to Shakespeare.

My religious life as a boy was suburban-evangelical. My spiritual home was my local 'Crusader Class'. Aged thirteen, I was 'converted' at a Tom Rees rally in the Albert Hall. (In the fifties Tom Rees was the nearest Britain had to Billy Graham.) Towards the end of a long emotionally overheated night, in response to the evangelist's closing appeal, I 'went forward' – I left my seat and went to the front. That was what you did on those occasions if you wanted to become a Christian. I was just showing off as usual.

Recently there was a huge rally in the Albert Hall to mark the one hundredth anniversary of the Crusaders Union (now known, inexplicably, as 'Urban Saints'). I would quite liked to have gone, if only because the programme featured 'BlushUK', a four-piece 'girl-band'. When I was a Crusader – and I wasn't much else in the fifties and sixties – girls were not allowed. Nor was the Church of England. Anglicans were, in our jargon, 'nominal Christians'. They weren't 'keen' like us. Their theology was 'woolly' and they indulged in what we called 'worldly amusements', such as the cinema and sherry. When I was fourteen I went into hospital for an operation. My Crusader leader – I am not making this up – gave me, for bedside reading, a huge Victorian edition of Fox's *Book of Martyrs*.

The big event in the Crusader calendar was summer camp. In

my day these camps were still organized like cantonments of the British army in India with commandants and canteen-wallahs, parades and padres, supernumeries and siestas. Much energy was devoted to eccentric sport. Halo, hacker, podex, crocker – each had its arcane rules on which the relevant 'wallah' had the final word. 'The spiritual side', as it was quaintly called, was the responsibility of the padre. Every evening in a big marquee, rollicking choruses were sung to the accompaniment of the hiss of Tilley lamps and the honky-tonk of a clapped-out piano. Then the padre – I was often one myself – would give an evangelistic talk. It was all horribly hearty but quite unemotional, I recall. The Holy Spirit only arrived some years later with the 'charismatic renewal' and after that things got a bit sticky. It was all most peculiar, but the movement still produced some notable Christian leaders, including several of today's bishops. And of course there is nothing peculiar about them. (My one regret is that I was never eligible for the famous 'Bash camps', the camps at Iwerne Minster organized by the Revd John Nash for the sons of the socially elevated. I am told that to qualify for a 'Bash camp' you had to get through an audition. You were asked to say 'Haileybury'. The ripe sound required – and the test was whether you had plums enough in your mouth to produce it – had to be one syllable.)

I was set on the path to the ordained ministry and the round-about road to Hackney by an eminent Victorian. Noel ('Tiny') Palmer was a towering four-year-old when Victoria died. When I met him fifty years later he was vicar of St John's, Bromley, the Anglican Church I had turned to after my Baptist boyhood. At six-foot-eight he was, as we feebly joked, the highest churchman in the Rochester diocese. Noel had been badly wounded on the Western Front in World War One. There, too, his public-school religion was blown to bits. Faith, hope, love – above all, love – were restored to him at Keswick, at the great convention of 1919 which some have spoken of as a second Pentecost. Up at Oxford, Noel befriended all and sundry, winning them for his Lord. He would have them all round to pray with him. In those days you prayed properly. You got up from your chair, turned round, and knelt at it. 'You can't go into Palmer's rooms without finding a forest of bottoms all over the place,' complained a fellow student.

The Victorians, taught by Thomas Carlyle, were unembarrassed by such heroes. Noel Palmer survived into an age that didn't know what to do with them. A new and nastier generation of evangelicals, with us to this day, suspected that he was 'unsound' and disowned him. The wounds he suffered in later life were as deep in their way as those he suffered on the Somme. But to the end his ringing laughter would still rattle the windows and his smile light up a cheerless room. Dear Noel. 'Many shall stand at the last day and call you blessed.'

Noel Palmer encouraged me to consider ordination. So did my bishop, the great Christopher Chavasse of Rochester. I was terrified by his accoutrements, his lorgnette-like cigarette-holder and his artificial leg with an alarming life of its own. But he gave me counsel which I only wish I had taken more to heart across the years. He told me that all that matters is my daily walk with God.

Once accepted for training, I resigned from my job with Legal & General. I had been working in their actuarial department, drafting company pension schemes. My career plan had been to become an actuary. Actuaries are people who find accounting too exciting. Actuaries calculate death rates. They know that nothing is for ever. That insight was to prove a comfort to me later when, so it came to feel, most of my work was 'striving officiously to keep alive' an institution which, like every other, is under sentence of death.

No longer a student actuary, I was immediately liable for National Service. Clergy fall into their groups, high or low, broad or narrow. Across the years I have become aware of an equally sharp and significant divide, the contrast between those who have done National Service and those born too late for it.

I think that I may have been the only priest in the Stepney episcopal area to have won a British Army prize for the use of the bayonet. The secret of success with the bayonet is to make such strange noises as you deploy it that your enemy is transfixed by astonishment long enough for you to stick it in him. 'The enemy' at the hour of my triumph was a sack of hay, hung from the branch of a tree at the barracks of the Royal West Kent regiment in Maidstone. Dexterity with the bayonet was all I learned – and the prize, a bag of apples, all I achieved – in my National Service. Otherwise my record was of abject failure. I never conquered my terror of the Company Sergeant-Major, the aptly named and permanently enraged Warrant-Officer Leech, whose comments on my turnout on parade turned my bowels to water. Needless to say, I failed my 'WOSBY', the War Office Selection Board. They had little difficulty in deciding I was not officer material. ('Private Pridmore, you have just marched your men into a minefield.')

No use to the infantry I was transferred, like hundreds of other faintly educated nincompoops, to the Intelligence Corps whose cap badge is 'a pansy resting on its laurels'. On the strength of a poor O level in German I was posted to Berlin to interrogate charwomen applying for cleaning jobs in sensitive military offices. Many a Frau Mop – now I can tell you – was not all she seemed. It was the Gilbert and Sullivan experience of National Service that largely explains why the culture of the Church of England a generation ago was so much more light-hearted and humane than it is today. Those two years had attuned us all to lunacy.

From the forces I went to Nottingham University to read theology. We were among the last to be undergraduates before John Henry Newman's *Idea of a University* had to be reclassified as a work of Victorian fantasy. There were giants in the land in those days. Our beloved professor, Alan Richardson, prophet of the now sadly defunct 'biblical theology' movement; the infinitely forbearing Robert Leaney, pundit on the Dead Sea Scrolls and the no-go areas at the back end of the Acts of the Apostles, and the author, so it was put about, of the children's classic *Happy Days with a Bucket and Spade in the Wadi Qumran*; the awesomely brilliant Richard

Hanson, so merciless on folly, so tender with fools; dear Molly Whitaker – never was one so learned, so self-effacing – who taught us New Testament Greek; Harry McKeating, whose cameo study of Noah entering the ark with a bottle under each arm delights me still. To be taught by such as these was an unparalleled privilege. Though there were scary moments. That first tutorial, for example, sitting in fear and trembling with another undergraduate, wondering what Richard Hanson would make of our juvenile essays on 'Abraham, Man or Myth?' Of course he was very nice to us. (The other student was a fresh-faced young chap straight from school called Hope. Whatever happened to him, I wonder?)

At Nottingham University I was still unpleasantly pious. I was President of the Christian Union, an organization which refused to affiliate with the University's 'Christian Association', the ecumenical body to which all the denominational organizations belonged. The 'CA' was, in our view, unsound and worldly. Members of the CA had been known to patronize the Student Union bars and to go to the dances held in the halls of residence on Saturday evenings. (This was long before students, saved and unsaved alike, took up clubbing.) For the avoidance of such occasions of sin, the CU set aside Saturday evenings for its 'Bible Readings'.

From Nottingham I went to Ridley Hall, Cambridge, where I began to thaw out theologically. The evangelicalism of Ridley in those days was temperate in its tone, civilized in its manners, and modest in its pretensions to scholarship. We were discouraged from overdoing it. There was much croquet, I recall. I revisited Ridley during my time in Hackney for a reunion of the former students of Cyril Bowles, the Hall's Principal from 1951 to 1963. They had to hire a marquee to accommodate us all. I'm sure that I wasn't the only one to gaze about me in wonder that so great a company of us were still, more or less, alive. It was all a great 'hoot' – to use a Ridley word – comparing notes about which bits of us still worked. And of course we exchanged memories of our dear Cyril who was so wise, so silent, so deep, so calm, and so kind. And,

11

in his own dry way, so very funny. I treasure still a typed invitation from him: 'Please come to the Principal's Lodge after Hall to meet the Ethiopian Abba.' To which note Cyril has added in his own hand, 'He is quite genuine.'

I was in chapel for that unforgettable Evensong when it gradually dawned on us, towards the end of Cyril's sermon, that he was about to break some news to us. The atmosphere was electric, not the usual climate in chapel in days when Anglican worship was so much more restful than it is now. Then the bombshell. Cyril told us that he had accepted the office of Archdeacon of Swindon. He could not have astonished us more had he announced that he had decided to become a Mormon or that he intended to resign his orders and train to be a chiropodist. Few of us had any idea what an Archdeacon did, but we were sure that it was way beneath our Cyril. And we didn't at all like the sound of Swindon.

Our reunion was a joyful but poignant occasion. My mind was haunted by Henry Scott Holland's famous account of Pusey's funeral: 'Up from every corner of the country came creeping the old men still left to whom his name had been a watchword and an inspiration . . . And as they turned away they knew that they would never meet again in such a company on this earth.'

I served my title in the parish of St Martin and St Meriadoc, Camborne, in the diocese of Truro, in the county of Cornwall, 'whose paths are worn by angels' feet'. I warm to Meriadoc who evangelized Cornwall, having sailed from Wales on a millstone. He too, surely, was a hobbit. My ministry began as it has continued, on a comic note. I was ordained by the saintly but eccentric Bishop Lash of Bombay. The attention of the bishop, his affection set on things above, seemed only partly engaged on the ceremonies over which he was presiding. When he lost the place his expedient was to intone the bidding 'Lift up your hearts'. While we all dutifully responded he would try to find out where we had got to.

After the service there was the usual bunfight. Someone gave me what looked like a rugby ball to eat. That was my first encounter with a Cornish pasty. I managed half of it. My attempt to flush the remainder down the church hall toilet could have brought my career as a clergyman to a close ten minutes after it had begun. The unconsumed portion wouldn't go round the bend. Perhaps it's still there. Somehow I got through the rest of the evening despite my terror that any moment a churchwarden might take me on one side and ask me for a quiet word.

My debt to Cornwall is deep. That obligation is, above all, to two saintly priests. The first was the incumbent who welcomed me to Camborne; the second was someone whom I never met, the minister of a remote Cornish parish in the 1920s and 1930s. One reason why, later on in Hackney, I refused to conform to the template of the disciplined and deferential modern clergyman was that I had known George Sandfield and had read about Bernard Walke. I recalled them both in my diary.

> Today at lunch five of my teeth fell out. 'The grinders cease because they are few.' I thought again of my first rector, the saintly Canon Sandfield of Camborne. I think a lot of him these days as things fall apart. Of him the tale told of many a parson was true. He really did propel his dentures from the pulpit into the lap of a lady in the front pew. I recall the first time I heard him preach. He'd just suffered the latest of a series of ghastly operations on his throat. He could barely whisper his text, 'We have this treasure in earthly vessels.' He died six weeks after my arrival in the parish. His was the first death I had witnessed. It was five in the morning. I wandered out of the ward. A cloudless sky was ablaze with stars. Close by – for the hospital to which they had taken him was near the cliffs – the sea beat on the rocks as it had done since time began. And I knew, I knew beyond all peradventure, that 'the end of sorrow shall be near the throne'.

> In the quiet days after Christmas I turn again to the book which, for me, above all others illuminates this holy season, Father Bernard Walke's *Twenty Years at St Hilary*.[2] When I was a curate in Cornwall a wonderful churchwarden (Mrs Rosewarne, of 'Little Rosewarne', Rosewarne) lent me a copy of Father Walke's book and reading it

13

confirmed my dawning awareness that I had come to a holy land. In Cornwall the veil between this world and another is very thin. For all my Christian agnosticism today, I do not doubt that the holiness of Cornwall has something to do with the story of a boy from Palestine who, they say, once visited its shores in the company of a tin-merchant, one Joseph of Arimathea. 'Christ came to Ding-Dong'. Bernard Walke would not have found that legend hard to believe. He was unconventional to a degree rare even among Cornish clergymen. He went everywhere on a donkey, believing that humanity's decline could be dated, not from the invention of the internal combustion engine, but from our decision to rush around everywhere on horseback. Previously he had been curate of Polruan where his cat ascended the pulpit with him when he was preaching, sitting by his notes on the reading stand. His bishop told him that 'good men were needed in the north'.

Each year Bernard Walke would gather the children of St Hilary and with them present the Christmas story as if it were all taking place in their own little parish. It was the broadcasting of this play in the early days of radio which, for a while, made St Hilary famous around the world. Some years ago I procured from the BBC sound archives a recording of the play. I no longer play this tape. It is too beautiful to bear, its poignancy the more piercing in the knowledge of how cruelly the St Hilary story came to an end. On the night of 9 August 1933 an extreme Protestant group came down from London in a charabanc and smashed the place up. 'The Kensitites' still claim that what they did to that lovely little church was legal. Perhaps it was. But they broke Father Walke's heart and angels no longer sing in the night sky above Relubbbas moor.

After Camborne I went back to Ridley Hall, as Tutor and Chaplain. (Several bishops and at least one archbishop have me to thank for the fact that they know the Greek for 'Behold, is that not a fish in the mouth of the apostle?') My four years back at Ridley were not the happiest in the Hall's history. That history is recorded in three volumes, F. W. B. Bullock's two-volume history,[3] which takes the story down to 1951, and Michael Botting's recently published third volume,[4] which brings the story into our own time. As I noted in my diary, Michael was kind enough to consult me about Ridley Hall as I had known it.

Bullock's *History of Ridley Hall, Cambridge* is a very boring book indeed, its tedium relieved only by its eccentrically chosen pictures ('The Association Football XI of 1896–7', 'The Visit of Mahatma Gandhi', 'The Hockey XI of 1924–1925'). Bullock, like the author of 2 Chronicles, had a passion for lists. ('Of the 462 Cambridge graduates, who came to Ridley while Tait was Principal, the following forty-six were Scholars of their Colleges . . .') His two-volume history stops in the early fifties. Now Michael Botting has written a third volume to bring the story up to date. His record of Ridley is a racier read. Michael asked me for my recollections of my time there as Chaplain. They are of somewhere far from boring. Barking maybe, boring never. The late sixties and early seventies saw the rise of the charismatic movement and Ridley Hall was one of the places where the Pentecostal fires flamed most fiercely. Those left legless by charismatic worship scorned the sobriety of what we churned out in chapel. Academic theology was dismissed as a dead letter by those alive in the spirit. The gift of tongues was more important than competence in New Testament Greek. A walnut tree outside the chapel came down one night prompting a wild-eyed prophet to announce that the end was nigh. A man turned up late to one of my tutorials because somebody on Kings Parade had to be 'delivered'. Some of us on the staff were also deemed to be demon-possessed. Bullock cannot match such drama – though he does tell us that in August 1927 the hall's waste pipes were renovated.

I left Ridley Hall to become a school chaplain for fifteen years. The school was the Bridewell Royal Hospital of King Edward's School, Witley, an establishment which began at the time of the Reformation as an asylum for the waifs and strays of London. Bishop Nicholas Ridley recognized these homeless children for who they were and, in a sermon preached before the teenage King Edward

VI, he pleaded for a home for them. As the bishop put it to the king, 'Christ hath been too long abroad on the streets of London.' So the boy-king gave his palace of Bridewell 'as a place to lodge Christ in'. That vision, of Christ the street-child, returned to challenge me when I arrived in Hackney, some of whose beggars are so very young.

I could write more about my years at King Edward's School and perhaps one day I will. Suffice it to say here that my chaplaincy to the young people whose lives I shared was guided by one theological principle. The Son of God, too, was once a troublesome teenager.

From King Edward's School, Witley, I went to Tanzania where I taught for two years in an International School. Its absurdly beautiful location was on the slopes of Mount Kilimanjaro. (I went to church occasionally, once to a confirmation service which, being Africa, went on for several hours. The bishop performed splendidly, except that he forgot the confirmation itself, the bit where he was supposed to 'lay hands' on the candidates one by one. Nobody seemed to notice or mind.)

Back from Africa, I spent a year on the now defunct ecumenical community based at Hengrave Hall in Suffolk. I had to cook lunch one day when Delia Smith, a trustee of Hengrave Hall, was our guest. Witnessing what I'd prepared, a wag on the community, quoting Scripture, asked 'Is there any taste in the slime of the purslane?'

In 1995 I was appointed as one of the curates at St Martin-in-the-Fields. St Martin-in-the-Fields is 'the greatest cure in England' and the most famous parish church in the world. It is also a reason not finally to despair of Anglicanism in its death throes. More importantly, St Martin-in-the-Fields has been the place where countless searching spirits have found their doubts and questions honoured and where they have been moved to gamble on the possibility that something behind the Christian story might be true. It was St Martin's that brought home to me again the principle that I had learned in Cornwall, that all our plans must be provisional. Parishes make their plans so that copies of them can be carefully filed in diocesan offices. What else they are for is less certain.

The reason that plans can never be more than provisional is that we never know what will happen next, or – if you like – what God will do next. St Martin's convinced me that this, so far from cynicism, is sober theology. 'What happened next' at St Martin's – and it would prove the same at St John-at-Hackney – was usually the unexpected. Here are a few miniatures from my diary recalling that most surprising of parish churches:

I was recently invited back to St Martin-in-the Fields. They asked me to preach on 'the power of the poor'. (I pleaded from the pulpit that this was like being asked to talk about 'the antiquities of Milton Keynes' or 'the charm of pigeons'.) Just before the service started a woman at the back began screaming obscenities. She was treated firmly but courteously and I was reminded again of why it is that St Martin-in-the-Fields is the best-loved parish church in Christendom. It is because it is a church where there are no strangers, only angels – some sadly fallen, no doubt, but still angels. That unscheduled introit was typical of countless contributions to the liturgy, not absolutely required by the rubric, which St Martin's has witnessed over the years. I was reminded of what happened one hot and sticky Sunday in my time there. While I was preaching a gentleman in the congregation rose to his feet, dropped his trousers, and raised his shirt to allow a little cooling air ('soft as the breath of even') to pass through the undergrowth. Thus refreshed he resumed his trousers and his seat. No one minded – but then all at St Martin-in-the-Fields have to undergo minor surgery to disable the muscles by which eyebrows are raised.

Palm crosses cascade down the steps of St Martin-in-the-Fields. It is the first anniversary of the outbreak of the genocide in Rwanda and the crosses, each one representing a hundred killed in the carnage, have been placed here by the aid agencies testifying together to the continuing plight of Rwanda. The impact of the image of this cataract of crosses is overpowering. Dwell on it – as many do throughout the day – and it becomes a river of blood. Rwanda – the very name is now, like Auschwitz, an emblem of atrocity. Once it was a name with other associations, speaking of spiritual fires burning in the hills of Africa, of tidal waves of blessing, of 'the most enduring revival of modern times'. How many there on the steps, I wondered, had heard of the Rwanda Revival? How many had heard of Algie Smith and of Len Sharp who kindled those flames? And how many would dare to trace the connection between Rwanda's Pentecost and its Passion?

It's been cold enough in the church of St John-at-Hackney this winter for bits of you to fall off without you noticing. The Siberian conditions have set me thinking about John the Baptist. I don't mean the hairy Judean with his diet – so a child once told me in a scripture exam – of 'crocuses and wild honey'. I have in mind a wonderful character, nicknamed John the Baptist, who during my spell at St Martin-in-the-Fields, spent his nights on the streets and his days sitting in the church. He always dressed the same way, wrapping himself in layer upon layer of plastic bin-liners. He had a curious shuffling walk, the reason for which became clear after his death when several hundred pounds in coins were discovered in his socks. I remember John the Baptist gratefully, as the water in our font freezes, for his advice on keeping warm in winter. The secret of survival, dear brother and sister, is what your grandmother taught you. Rub your chest liberally with lard.

For all our ringing declarations about marriage, the punters still miss the point. One Saturday at St Martin's the verger called me to say that there was a couple with him who wanted to get married. I hurried across to the church to have a chat with them, only to find that the man already had a buttonhole in his best suit and that the woman was wearing a wedding dress. Apparently they'd supposed that all you had to do to get married in church was to turn up. They were most put out to learn that it wasn't quite that simple. 'We've got a witness,' they protested. At which point as melancholy a figure as I have ever encountered emerged from the shadows. As the couple departed in a huff he whispered mournfully in my ear, 'They'll regret this on the day of Armageddon.'

Back to St Martin-in-the-Fields – or at least to the pub next door – on All Saints Day. We gather, a raffish crew, in the seedy upper room of the Marquis of Granby. The faithful of St Martin's are loyal to their local. Instances of overindulgence after evensong, though not unheard of, are rare. We're all old friends of William, for many years the St Martin's archivist. We are here to raise a glass to him on his birthday (and, as it happens, mine) and to listen to a talk from him about the legendary Dick Sheppard, Vicar of St Martin's during the First World War. Dick died, universally loved and utterly alone, on the eve of All Saints Day, 1937. Still we seek his secret. Tonight there is much talk about what might have been. What would have become of Dick's pacifism had he survived to experience the Second World War? What if his wife had returned to him, as they say she was about to when he died? Supposing they could have done something for his asthma and his crippling depressions? All these 'What ifs'. Mine is more far-fetched. I ask what we'd make of Dick if he came back today. I remind people of the last scene of George Bernard Shaw's *St Joan* where Joan appears in a vision. They all pay their fulsome tributes to her until, aghast, they hear her threatening to come back to them a living woman. And Dunois says to Joan: 'Forgive us. We are not yet good enough for you. I shall go back to bed.'

After five years at St Martin's it was time to take on a parish. The path to Hackney took one last comic twist. Richard Chartres, then Bishop of Stepney, suggested that I had a look at St John's. So we drove over to Hackney to spy out the land. From what we could see from the outside, we liked the look of the church and rectory, pleasantly situated at the edge of a park. All else being equal, we thought we'd take it on. Back at our flat in Trafalgar Square, we checked the London *A–Z*. We'd been looking at the wrong St John's – St John of Jerusalem not St John-at-Hackney. Sometimes I wearily wish that I did not so often make such an ass of myself. I console myself with the thought that the good Lord was fond of donkeys.

Life at St Martin-in-the-Fields was the experience of 'the trivial transfigured'. It is the pattern of the incarnation, of 'a poor bare forked animal' possessed by divinity. So it would be in Hackney, where the ridiculous would often be overtaken by the sublime. That is what happened one Saturday night and Sunday morning. What took place can serve as an overture for the rest of this book.

5.00 pm Saturday. A white van draws up outside Marks and Spencers, just across the road from our rectory. Several young men jump out. One of them unloads a huge sound-system which is soon causing the ground to tremble and doing damage to my eardrums. His colleagues – large men whom it is hard to refuse – are pressing leaflets on passers-by, invitations to attend a 'free gospel concert' later tonight. Aware of the fragility of the rectory porcelain, I decide – if I can make myself heard – to say something. So I bellow into an enormous ear, 'You are committing a public nuisance!' 'Unless you turn to Jesus, you will go to hell!' he of the cauliflower ear retorts. Such is the infernal noise he's making, I feel I'm half way there already.

7.00 pm Saturday. I wander round the garden, watering the beds I should be weeding. But the peace I crave is not to be. There's a loud crump as something lands in the bushes behind me. A furious voice from over the wall shouts, 'Where are those DVDs? Come on! Where are they?' I drop the hose and hurry out the back gate. A policeman has a Vietnamese lad up against our garden wall. I am torn between a public-spirited wish to assist the police with their enquiries and sympathy with a poor man evidently in need of a wash and a meal. Another policeman appears at the double. Not wanting the chap coming back later and roaming round our garden, I tell the police what I heard. Back in the garden there's no need for sniffer-dogs. We quickly find a Tesco bag stuffed with pirated DVDs. The constabulary, armed with the evidence, leads the youth away. For some reason I feel ashamed of myself.

11.00 pm Saturday. One more thing to do before going to bed. That's to turn off the hose. I clamber over the domestic detritus in our garage to reach the tap. I turn the tap – and the whole bloody thing blows apart. A great geyser shoots to the ceiling. I try replacing the tap and only succeed in improvising a powerful water-cannon which drenches me. Again and again I try to force the tap back on. I hear sad little whimpering noises. There's no one else in the garage, so it must be me. The floods rise about me. I cry out with Job, 'Terrors take hold on me as waters' (Job 27.50). Finally I slosh indoors and eventually get through on the phone to an emergency plumber. 'Can't get to you for another hour,' he says, with that inimitable intake of breath they teach you at plumbing school. He tells me to turn off my stopcock. It is an injunction I cannot obey for the simple reason that I have no idea where it is.

1.00 am Sunday. The plumber arrives and ten minutes later the problem is solved. Before he passes into the night, having pocketed a large slice of my month's stipend, he says something which gives me pause: 'I find that people are afraid of water.' He's right, of course. It is our primal fear. Why otherwise the promise that one day 'there shall be no more sea'?

2.00 am Sunday. A restless night (the little left of it). I lie awake nursing a sense of shame. My head is an attic full of junk, a repository of useless information. I can point you to both places in *The Book of Common Prayer* where the rubric 'or this' occurs. I know that John Keble's sister had a wooden leg. I remember that in classical Hebrew there is something called an 'unassimilated nun energic'. But such snippets will not save me at the last dread visitation when I am banished to hell's nethermost circle where languish those wretched clergy who did not know where their stopcocks were.

7.30 am Sunday. I'm only half awake and only half listening to the 'Sunday' programme on Radio 4. The snatches I hear do not improve my temper. This morning the lead story, so far as I can make out, is something about the Bishop of Sydney, who it seems has boarded up the stained-glass windows in his churches, exchanged his altars for filing-cabinets, and replaced Choral Evensong with public readings from the Collected Works of the Reverend Professor Dr James Packer. Sometimes, as today, the cast of the 'Sunday' programme is nothing but a cavalcade of crackpots. But we shouldn't be surprised. As Harry Williams taught us long ago, 'Religion is what men do with their lunacy.'

11.00 am Sunday. Our Parish Communion draws to a close. Our way of doing things here is 'very Hackney' and would appal the purists. But somehow it has worked, as it usually does. Something wonderful has happened. All the little sadnesses, absurdities, and follies that have preoccupied me over the last twenty-four hours have been brought to the Holy Table and dealt with. These irritations are far less important than the delightful people I say goodbye to at the door. No doubt next Sunday there will be other tribulations, grave or comic, which will have to be 'tabled' in the same way. Meanwhile I tell myself, as I stroll home for lunch, that this is a good place to be.

3

Hackney Ancient and Modern

The queue in our local Post Office is endless but you learn a lot about Hackney as you wait in it. Someone has pushed to the front. The queue is loud in protest. A clerk behind the counter, appointed for her sanctity, tries to pacify a bellicose customer who thinks he's been diddled. The queue is less patient than she is. Moments later she is courteously declining the overtures of a gentleman – no stranger to the lager can, alas – who, while waiting for his Giro, has apparently fallen in love with her. On balance the queue is of the view that they are unsuited. Now a woman is complaining bitterly to her neighbour of the failure of our Health Centre to take her symptoms seriously. The queue by contrast is fascinated by them. A young man on a mobile phone forgets he has an audience. 'I gave all that up, man, when I came to Jesus'. The queue wishes he would be more specific. So the drama unfolds until at last a bright voice announces, 'Cashier number five, please!'

Samuel Pepys enjoyed riding out to Hackney with his wife 'to take the ayre', not a purpose that brings many to Hackney these days. In Pepys's day Hackney was still a village. Its hayfields fed the horses that kept London's traffic moving. Its fresh streams provided clean water for the big city. Tescos car-park, where today you purchase your pirated DVDs, was once a watercress farm. Since the Middle Ages Hackney had been home to wealthy merchants and courtiers. Sutton House, an imposing Tudor building and at one time the church hall, is the grandest of Hackney's old houses. (It is just across the road from what, until its timely closure, was one of the toughest comprehensive schools in London.) Hackney was a posh place. Daniel Defoe said of Hackney that 'there are more coaches than Christians in it'. The area's former prosperity is evidenced by the handsome table tombs around the parish church, with their florid tributes to the worthies whose remains they house. Admiral Beaufort, famous for his Beaufort scale, rests here. Today you will often see one of Hackney's homeless bedding down with the dead in the ruins of one or other of these old tombs.

Well into the Victorian period Hackney retained its character as a superior neighbourhood where the leisured and elevated settled. Then the railway came. Then came the industries. The 'ayre', so enjoyed by Pepys, was rendered less inviting by the opening of Berger's paint factory and Carless Capel & Leonard's chemicals plant. Rows and rows of prim houses were built – and some not so prim. The fields disappeared. Hackney ceased to be as green and pleasant as once it was. Many of Hackney's well off moved to what they deemed to be more salubrious neighbourhoods.

The twentieth century saw a steep decline in Hackney's fortunes. Nice little houses deteriorated into slums and when those slums were demolished they were replaced by bleak estates and grim tower blocks with lifts that broke down. Factories closed in Hackney, as they closed everywhere else. (One of the last to go had made small boys of every age happy, Lesney's Matchbox Toys factory.) The businesses that took their place were at the seedier end of the market, scrap-merchants, dodgy second-hand car dealers, and the like. In recent years some of the worst tower blocks have been demolished and the more hideous of the estates refurbished. But life on an estate can still be unpleasant, especially when kids have urinated on the live power cables in the basement of your block, plunging your home in darkness.

Notoriously, Hackney Council in the 1980s was run by the 'loony left'. The council ended its twinning arrangements with France, West Germany and Israel and set up new links with the Soviet Union, East Germany and Nicaragua. Hackney in those days was *tohu-wa-bohu*. *Tohu-wa-bohu* is the Hebrew for primal chaos. According to Genesis that is how things were before God said 'Let there be light'. In those days Hackney's finances were spectacularly *tohu-wa-bohu.* Annual multimillion pound deficits were black holes swallowing any hope of better days. Rubbish mounted in the streets. There were massed protests outside the Town Hall. The rotting fabric of council housing went unrepaired. Some council tenants were unable to pay their rents because the council was failing to pay their housing benefits – which of course did not stop the council threatening them with eviction. Poor old Hackney.

For all Hackney's continuing problems, those dark days are done. Hackney Council is slowly dealing with the legacy of its past ineptitude. The council is no longer 'a zero-rated' authority and the worst performing in the country. The government mandarins that measure these matters report that the borough is 'improving well'. But to this day the Town Hall has never quite lost its reputation as a hive of crackpots. It is a burden that those who work there today, most of whom have no need of being sectioned, have to bear as best they can.

As late as my arrival in Hackney in 1995, there were occasional reminders of what my neighbours in Hackney had had to suffer across the years. I noted one chilling experience in my diary:

I call in at my local GP's to register. We are told that the National Health Service is near collapse. I don't know about that. I do notice that the doorway to my doctor's, approached through a tide of litter, is propped up by a Heath Robinson arrangement of rusting scaffolding and that the ceiling of the waiting room is supported in the same way. The receptionist would need little time to change before appearing onstage as Mrs Habershon. I notice too the manky wallpaper, the scrofulous threadbare carpets, the smell of damp and decay unconquered by the vapours of the single Calor gas heater. This wretched room has not been redecorated for a generation. Perhaps it would not seem so awful if I had not called at another surgery earlier, premises as bright and welcoming as these are drab and repelling – but that was to see the vet about getting the cat wormed. The possibility worries me that in a year or two's time I shall no longer be shocked by what Hackney people have to put up with.

Since the Second World War, many from far away have settled in Hackney. Some of them have become British citizens. Today they take part in a 'Citizenship Ceremony' in the Town Hall, a ceremony in which Hackney's history of welcoming newcomers is affirmed:

> 'Hackney has been for centuries a place that has respected points of view that are different from the mainstream; a place to which people have come to find refuge from the family and social pressures of being in some way different. We are a non-conformist borough and that's part of what makes Hackney a good place to live in.'

Whether everyone in Hackney has always been equally welcoming of the stranger is debatable. Pockets of mistrust of 'the other' certainly persist, as we shall see. But the Town Hall is quite right to take some pride in how well the different groups rub along with each other. It is something Hackney children have to learn at school. I kept on file a report on our church secondary school's 'Ethnic Minority Achievement Success'. The report listed the different 'first languages' spoken by our pupils – Yoruba, Twi, Cantonese, Krio, Okpe, Vietnamese, Punjabi, Creole, Ibo, Edo, Urdu, Lingala, Russian, Hindi, Turkish – and many, many more. The document is a window on to the world of worlds which was my incomparable parish.

From the 1950s many of Afro-Caribbean descent came to live in Hackney. (Though there were black people in Hackney well before then. The parish burial register records that one 'Anthony, a poore old negro' died in 1630. He was 105.) Most of the West Indians who settled in Hackney were devout Christians. So, too, were many of the Nigerians who made their homes among us. Not all of them were made welcome in our white churches. It is testimony to their Christian forbearance that so many of them put up with us as long as they did. Others gave up on us and so began the 'Black majority churches' of our inner cities. These days, of course, the Anglican churches of our inner cities are predominantly black as well, as too are the Methodist and other nonconformist churches.

There is a big community of Turkish people in Hackney. In my first years as Rector of Hackney I looked after two churches. These churches stand at either end of Hackney's 'murder mile' – more of which in the next chapter. When I walked between my two churches I passed a dozen Turkish shopfront coffee houses, each with its pool table, TV from Turkey, and men playing interminable games of cards. The Turkish Muslim community is served by their magnificent and admirably hospitable mosque on the Kingsland Road. Built in the 1990s, it is the only religious building in Hackney bigger than the church of St John-at-Hackney. Not only is it bigger, it is far better planned. And, unlike St John-at-Hackney, its dome doesn't leak.

Jews have always lived in Hackney. 25,000 Hasidic Jews, in their distinctive garb, live in Stamford Hill, the third largest such community in the world. Only in Israel and New York are there more *hasidim*. For much of my time the borough had a Jewish mayor, the splendid Joe Lobenstein ('the one-man dynasty of Hackney politics'). I mentioned him in my diary.

After the Second World War many Jews moved up into Hackney from the heart of the old East End. Now most have moved on and the remaining congregations are aging and dwindling. To be sure, the ultra-orthodox are there in large numbers in the north of the borough, but many of Hackney's old synagogues have been demolished. However Hackney does have to be deeply grateful to its Jewish mayor. He is strictly orthodox. He won't enter a church or indeed shake hands with half of us – not even with the Queen when she recently visited the Homerton Hospital. But he has been re-elected for an unprecedented fourth term and his commitment to the flourishing of all races and all faiths in Hackney has been exemplary. There may well have been political reasons too for his long tenure but there's no doubt that 'his lightness of touch and generosity in conducting council meetings' (I quote the words of a local vicar who is also a councillor) have gone far to prevent hostilities in the council chamber turning into all-out war.

The good news is that Jews are returning to Hackney, and not just to Stamford Hill. A new synagogue is being built adjacent to a disused Jewish burial ground in South Hackney. Protests were made at the planning stage that the development would mean lots of cars with nowhere to park. Those raising that complaint had to be reminded that Orthodox Jews are forbidden to drive on the Sabbath. (Another daft objection swiftly overruled was that people coming and going would disturb any bats nesting in the nearby trees.)

Hackney's 'Citizenship Ceremony' claims that Hackney has always been 'a nonconformist borough'. True. As we shall see, the large population of dissenters in Hackney in the eighteenth century was perceived by the established church as a threat. There is one nonconformist associated with Hackney who was never far from my mind while I was in the parish. I was reminded of him each day taking my daughter to school. Up the road from Del Boys Bagels, just past the Burberry's factory shop, much patronized by Japanese tourists, is the site of the Old Gravel Pit Meeting House. Here, on 8 March 1851, the Scottish story-teller George MacDonald married his Hackney sweetheart Louisa Powell. I wrote about their wedding in my diary.

The bridegroom sported a satin waistcoat embroidered with sprigs of flowers. The white scarf worn by the bride still had the price tag on it. The next day – no one seemed to think this odd – MacDonald was to preach in Rugby. Unpacking their luggage on arrival in Rugby, MacDonald found that a bottle of cod liver oil had smashed in his suitcase ruining his best trousers. George and Louisa were married for fifty-four years and had eleven children of their own ('the wrong side of a dozen'). Then they adopted two more. MacDonald's wedding gift to his wife was a poem, not one of his best.

Love me beloved; for both must lie
Under the earth and beneath the sky
The world be the same when we are gone
The leaves and the waters all sound on . . .

George and Louisa's ashes are mingled in the warm soil of a Mediterranean churchyard. We fly forgotten as a dream. And I must hurry on or Rebecca will be late for school.

We shall meet George MacDonald again.

Three developments in recent years have altered the Hackney's social profile. Three groups of people have arrived, or emerged, in large numbers: the artists, the upwardly mobile, and the villains The villains can wait until the next chapter

Lately Hackney has become something of an artists' colony. Few of Hackney's many galleries are as prestigious and successful as Hoxton's 'White Cube'. Not all local artists have done as well as Sophie Dickens (great-great-granddaughter of Charles Dickens), winner in 2007 of the Victoria and Albert Museum's Founders' Prize. Her studio is a small garage on one of Hackney's huge estates. Most of the tiny studios, potteries and workshops that abound in the borough survive, if they do, on a shoestring. But for those who see that there is more to be made than the next buck, the presence of so many artistic people about the place makes Hackney an exciting place to live. It is the opulent but monochrome City and the dreary dormitory suburbs that make the heart sink.

Hackney attracts musicians. For some years the Hackney Youth Orchestra rehearsed and performed in our church. I wish we had welcomed too The Zimmers, Hackney's octogenarian rock band. The Zimmers believe in 'growing old disgracefully'. They strengthen my conviction that it is never too late to have a misspent youth.

Hackney fascinates film people. Location managers love its lively markets, its seedy estates, its sinister canals. Above all, they constantly return to Hackney Marshes. Every day of the year a TV or film shoot is taking place somewhere in Hackney. There is an office in the Town Hall to assist the film-makers and to relieve them of fat facility fees. I had lots of requests for permission to film in our churchyard and I was unfailingly hospitable to enquirers with cheque books.

But there were creative people in Hackney long before the film crews arrived. Hackney's older artistic heritage is its tradition of the music hall performer and the circus clown. The Hackney Empire, the last of the great East End music halls, has now been restored to its original splendour. Alas, in the process it has lost something of its former glory. (A *Guardian* columnist refers to its 'self-consciously scrubbed-up look'.) I wrote in my diary about an instructive evening at the Empire soon after my arrival in the parish and long before it was refurbished.

> *King Lear* is being staged in the decomposing splendours of the Hackney Empire. The Hackney Empire is not, as some jokers in the deanery would have it, the Hackney Team Ministry. It is the East End's last and most magnificent music hall, the supreme achievement of theatre-builder Frank Matcham whose apprentice work includes the London Coliseum. It is a gilt and scarlet riot of decaying domes and mouldering drapes, of crumbling plaster *putti* and peeling paint. Some funding has been found – and much more is sought – for its refurbishment. But of course the place won't be half as charming when it is as good as new. Restoration can be the ruin of old masters and I am glad to have seen the Hackney Empire in its sumptuous decline. It is a fitting setting for the tragedy of a derelict king who forfeits his right to rule but who still insists on dressing up and sitting on a throne. This production, in which Warren Mitchell plays Lear, is by far the most intelligent reading of the play I have seen. *King Lear* is, famously, 'a Christian play about a pagan world'. We have always known that it is a play about the possibility of redemptive suffering. Perhaps it is also about an established church still secretly in love with the rococo trappings of the power it no longer holds, a church that may yet be forced to exchange its strongholds for the wilderness and to find its true identity beneath the bare branches of a cross.

Lear's companion in the wilderness was his 'all-licensed fool'. Hackney loves holy fools. (Perhaps that is why Hackney is kind to its clergy.) A neighbouring parish church, All Saints, Haggerston, is London's 'Clowns' Church'. When Zippo's Circus came to Victoria Park I wrote in my diary:

> I sing 'the great spheral circus-song and the undying glory of the Ring.' Zippo's Circus was back again this year in Vicky Park and we had ringside seats. I'm thinking of settling down to write a book on 'Circus as Sacrament'. The circus, like the Mass itself, exposes the frontier we draw between the phenomenal and the real for the mischievous fiction it is. A good circus, like Zippo's, alters irreversibly our perception of the universe. Nothing can be the same again. (And unlike church only the dogs, not the children, have to jump through hoops to take part.) It is above all the clowns who alert us to the divine comedy of our humdrum lives. Zippo's has a gloriously lugubrious clown with huge feet and ears. My wife tells me that he looks like me.

There are lots of artists in Hackney looking for places to exhibit their work. I regret that we did not make the most of our church as an exhibition space. As its cavernous interior is on the same scale as that of the Turbine Hall at the Tate Modern, it would be ideal for the vast installations that are so popular these days. Perhaps we should not have turned down an opportunity to display the work of one artist who raises eyebrows.

> In the end it wasn't the pickled sheep but we've still had to say no. It all began with our being asked whether we had the wall-space in our church to display some pictures as part of a 'Millennium Art Trail' through East London. 'Fine', we said. After all, wall-space is what we do have lots of. (Converts no, wall-space yes.) Now I am told that we'd been put down to hang thirteen Damien Hirsts. In the event we'd not been assigned his sliced livestock suspended in formaldehyde. At first sight what they were offering – I have the illustrations in front of me – look like huge blow-ups of labels from bottles you buy

31

at Boots. But these are not for Paracetamol and the like. Instead we have, 'Omelette – 10 tablets', 'Sausages – 4 capsules', 'Steak and Kidney – 100 tablets', 'Liver, Bacon, Onions (for intracardiac and intravenous use)', and so on and on. And the whole series is entitled 'The Last Supper'. The exhibition, an accompanying hand-out tells me, is to 'explore deep-rooted universal themes: creation, redemption and liberation'. I thought of a story about an emperor's new clothes.

None of the artists at work in Hackney is as wealthy as Damien Hirst, but recent years have seen an influx of young professional people into the neighbourhood who aspire to be. On Saturday mornings they shop in the Broadway Market for foodstuffs unknown to earlier East Enders – lime cheese, wild boar sausages, orange rye pumpernickel, and the like. It is no longer impossible to buy a café latte in Hackney. There are not yet as many stylish wine bars as there are 'greasy spoons' and Burger Kings, but soon there will be. 'Hackney Central' is a railway station, but it is also one of those new wine bars. To step inside it is to enter an ambience that owes nothing to Hackney and everything to the appetites and tastes of the affluent anywhere.

More threatening to Hackney's poor are the spiralling house prices. Such prices are spare cash for those on huge salaries and gross bonuses in the City twenty minutes away. They are the ones targeted by the developers who buy up crumbling properties – old council schools, the premises of bankrupt businesses, disused warehouses and the like – and turn them into luxury apartments. The limited 'affordable' social housing available in Hackney is anything but affordable if you are on a below-average income. In Hackney, as in all our inner-city areas, 'gentrification' is a wedge driving still further apart the haves and have-nots. It has little to do with the 'regeneration' of poor places. It has still less to do with what Christians call resurrection.

Talking of Hackney Central, something must be said about the trains that stop there – and, more worryingly, those that don't stop there.

If ever I choose to end it all by throwing myself under a train it will be on that most dismal of lines, the North London Railway. I rarely ride it, for we must not invite more than our allotted sorrows. The line reminds me of the old Berlin S-Bahn, a network of dilapidated track running between East and West along which an occasional derelict and verminous train trundled carrying a sad assortment of defectors, small-time spies, and smugglers of long-playing gramophone records. By day the NLR's infrequent and unpunctual service allows you, should you have so little purpose in life to wish to do so, to travel from Frognal to North Woolwich. By night its more sinister function is fulfilled. The line runs near enough to our Rectory for its traffic to be audible in the early hours. As I lie awake wondering how to look after ten thousand souls and a leaking church roof I hear them rumbling by, the waggons of nuclear waste destined for Sellafield and, after infernal processes, for the arming of nuclear warheads. The death-rattle of the trucks resonates with the dark tenor of my thoughts and I cry for the dawn.

Hackney Parish Church has been at the heart of Hackney's history for generations. However in recent years the ties between parish church and local community have been loosened. That is just as it should be, for in a multicultural neighbourhood the church can no longer claim any privileged status over mosque or synagogue, gudwara or temple, although some in ecclesiastical high places act as if it were not so. The status of the church in society is slowly slipping. Perhaps if it carries on slipping long enough, it will end up where it should have been all along, alongside one who was despised and rejected by everyone.

Certainly much has changed at St John-at-Hackney since it was last visited by a royal.

Hackney Parish Church has been visited by the Prince of Wales. Not recently, it has to be said, but in 1921. Someone's just sent me, scavenged from a loft, a copy of the illustrated souvenir edition of the parish magazine celebrating his visit. The rector of the day contributes a gushing editorial. 'The prince possesses the simple natural grace that is the mark of true manhood . . . The Empire is fortunate indeed in possessing such a man as heir to the throne.' A church-warden, writing on 'loyalty', loses his drift. 'Our patriotism is as a religion, of which the King is as a Sacrament.' There are several photographs of the Prince, dressed in all of them like the Great Gatsby. Among them, for some reason I cannot fathom, is a picture of him chatting with the Notts County goalkeeper. As always with parish magazines it is the small ads which yield the gems. Fowler and Piggin are now showing 'all the latest novelties in hosiery'. Prendergasts will adjust your sewing machine and Rose and Sons will pay a fair price for the insides of your old eiderdown. Nappers have 'the largest stock of Dorothy-bags in the district'. Clarnicos tell us that their cream caramels 'cannot be compared with anything except themselves'. Perhaps that is why they went out of business.

For a brief period the history of Hackney Parish Church became part of the larger story of church and state. Sunday 30 January 2005 was the one hundred and fiftieth anniversary of the death of the man who gave St John-at-Hackney its place in history. They nicknamed Joshua Watson 'Arch-Treasurer Watson', such was his way with money, whether his own wealth from the wine trade or the fortune he raised to finance his countless good works. Watson was the leader of 'the Hackney Phalanx', the coterie of high church-men who in the early nineteenth century paved the way for the Tractarians. At a meeting in his mansion overlooking Clapton Pond, Watson and his friends in the Phalanx founded 'the National Society for the Promotion of the Education of the Poor in the Principles of the Established Church'. Watson was the powerhouse behind such worthy causes as the Clergy Orphan Society, the London Fever Hospital, and the Society for the Suppression of Vice.

Watson – a child of his time – thought that bishops were a good thing and created a chain of colonial bishoprics from Calcutta to Nova Scotia. He was just as keen on curates and started the Additional Curates Society. Mistrustful of mavericks, Watson was not sure what to make of the young John Henry Newman. In his opinion the *Tracts for the Times* should have been edited by a committee. He was implacably opposed to Protestant dissent and disliked Bunyan's *Pilgrim's Progress*. William Cobbett loathed Watson. 'Oh! Joshua Watson!' he wrote. 'Alas! Wine and spirit merchant who art head of a Society for Promoting Christian Knowledge . . .' On the morning of the anniversary of his passing the present secretary of the Additional Curates Society placed a beautiful wreath on his tomb in our churchyard. By sunset, such is Hackney, it had gone.

Joshua was the brother of John Watson, Rector of Hackney for forty years. While I was rector, memorials to the two brothers frowned down on me from either side of the sanctuary. Theirs was something of a Martha and Mary relationship. Joshua was hyperactive in good works. I never was able to discover quite what his brother, the rector, did. (My parishioners may have had a similar problem.) I like to think that he was a 'man of prayer' and as such the power behind his more famous brother.

There was a portrait of John Watson, alongside many other pictures of previous rectors, on my vestry wall. One of my bad tempered diary entries – made about the time we were bombarded with bumph about *Common Worship* – refers to this gallery.

My predecessors stare reproachfully down on me as the service is about to start. I am still faffing about with the radio-mike, banns-book, sermon notes, and all the other impedimenta that a priest more worthy of his calling would have organized an hour ago. By this stage Archdeacon Pink – there he is, up there over the door – whose ministry here half a century ago is often recalled, much to my disadvantage, would certainly have been deep in his preparatory devotions. But the picture I would most like to puncture with poisoned darts is that of the Revd. Frederick Gardiner, Rector of Hackney in the 1890s, and his four elegant curates. All have adopted statuesque poses and stare coldly into the distance. It is as if they are awaiting the return of our Lord but are fearful that he might not be a nice class of person. Four curates, one of whom, I am told, was the Rector's personal domestic chaplain. Now we have no curate and there is small prospect of getting one. I would not mind that if it were not for the endless admonitions and intimations from the ever more powerful 'centre'. For example, my keen clergy friends who keep abreast of all this paperwork tell me that I am expected to introduce a whole raft of new services soon. Who is going to mind the shop, I wonder, while I try to get my head round those? On this matter I shall seek the all-prevailing intercession of the late Archdeacon Pink.

I am fascinated by another clergyman in Hackney's history who certainly spent little time saying his prayers. The tiny chapel attached to our seventeenth-century almshouse, founded by Bishop Thomas Wood, has been claimed to be 'the smallest consecrated church in the land'. The almshouse was built to house 'ten poor ancient widows'. Their chapel had ten oak stalls and ten straw stools and with all ten ancients present the place was full up.

There was a piece about Bishop Wood in a recent issue of *Hackney History*. He was not, it seems, an adornment to the bench. He had been chaplain to Charles I and then – bouncing back after the Commonwealth – to Charles II. Under the latter his career really took off. One hundred pounds in a brown envelope secured him the Deanery of Lichfield. His bishop immediately excommunicated him, 'causing the sentence to be read in the cathedral while Wood was in church'. Excommunicated or not, when the bishop died Wood succeeded him. Gossip had it that this further advancement was thanks to the pillow-talk of Barbara Villiers ('the lewdest as well as the fairest of all King Charles's concubines') with whom Wood was advantageously acquainted. Once consecrated as Bishop of Lichfield, Wood promptly pocketed the money provided for his palace and retired to Hackney where he continued to live off his vast diocesan revenues. When ordered to return to his see he promised to do so 'when the weather was somewhat cooler'.

In the end the Archbishop of Canterbury suspended him. His

handsome tomb is in St John-at-Hackney church. But the old reprobate, for whom I confess a sneaking admiration, has another memorial. The little almshouse which he founded and which bears his name flourishes to this day. Take a 38 bus to Clapton Ponds and you are there.

Hackney has at least four churches dedicated to one or other of the Johns honoured in the Christian calendar. Traditions already old when Hackney was still a village are maintained in one of them. We were there very early one Easter Day.

On the stroke of midnight the Holy Door of the Iconostasis is flung open and the Easter fire is carried into the body of the Church. Its single flame pierces the total darkness. The great cry 'Christos aneste' – 'Christ is risen' – is taken up and repeated by the vast congregation. Each of us is carrying an unlit candle. From that one flame the fire is passed, candle to candle, until the dark house is full of light. Joy is come again. This is not on Mount Athos or at the aedicule of the Holy Sepulchre in Jerusalem but half-a-mile up the road in the Greek Orthodox church of Saint John the Theologian. The ancient liturgy makes no concession whatever to contemporary culture. No wonder the place is packed.

4

Murder Mile

'There are possibly more shots discharged in this area than anywhere
else in Britain.' So says *The Observer*. For those who don't know
Hackney there's a map with cheerful little stars on it to show you
where seven people have been shot dead in recent years. It's a map of
my parish. The Lower Clapton Road, which links the two churches of
our team, has been dubbed Britain's 'murder mile'. There have been
these seven 'gangland executions', but no one is keeping a record of
all the other occasions when guns have been drawn and fired. And no
one in this terrified neighbourhood is naming names. The old ladies
in our almshouses, just across the road from the sinister nightclub
that has been the scene of several of the shootings, ask me if they can
have a padlock on their front gate. 'Life is cheap in Hackney,' the
owner of a local kebab shop tells me. I listen to the dispassionate
observations of a mother whose boy has been murdered and I am distressed by her equanimity. Just as I am disturbed by the unruffled
manner of the Dad who calls on me today asking for copies of the
baptism certificates of his five children. He mentions – but only in
passing – that, with their mother, they all perished in an arson attack
on his home. There are things going on round here to which I find it
hard to adjust.

In 2006 a Channel 4 programme branded Hackney as Britain's
'worst place to live'. I do not agree with this damning verdict. I wear
my 'I love Hackney' T-shirt with pride. But I can see why those for
whom statistics are sacred might make that judgement. Those
statistics, for what they're worth, tell us that four out of ten in
Hackney of working age are unemployed, that most children leave
school with GCSE results way below the national average, and that
a third of Hackney's population live in overcrowded homes. More

people in Hackney suffer from schizophrenia than in any other London inner-city borough. In 2007 Hackney was hit by the biggest outbreak of measles seen anywhere in the UK for years. Demands on social services provision are massive. Many have fallen through the welfare net. Hackney bumps along the bottom of any table of social well-being you care to consult. A year or two ago a young man, for whom it had all got too much, jumped off one of the local tower blocks. The next day another young man, apparently thinking that this was a good way to solve your problems, jumped off the same tower block and ended his life on the same spot.

But for the makers of the Channel 4 programme the side of Hackney life which makes it such an unattractive place to live, more than any other of its alleged shortcomings, is its criminality. Once upon a time it was the left-wing lunacy of its Town Hall that earned Hackney its notoriety. Today it is not the dottiness of civic Trots which tarnishes Hackney's reputation but the level of violent crime on its streets, especially of gun-crime. I turn to the *Hackney Gazette*. The front-page headline is 'Gunmen strike in rush hour attack'. The incident took place a couple of hundred yards from what was my rectory. A car 'containing several youths wearing masks' pursues a blue Toyota, forcing it to crash into a lamp-post. A gunman gets out of the pursuing car and fires several shots into the crashed vehicle. Miraculously neither of the occupants of the car, a man and a thirteen-year old boy, is killed. That was one week's lead story, but it echoes many others splashed across the front page of our local press in recent years.

Such front page news in the *Hackney Gazette* is no more depressing than what is reported on its inner pages. As I write, the headline in the latest *Gazette* is 'Teenage rapist caged'. I open the paper and the by-lines catch my eye – 'Second man on murder charge', 'Smashed with brick', 'Teen's face slashed', 'Toilet death', 'Teenager hurt in hammer attack', 'Conmen prey on elderly', 'Woman stabbed in row with neighbour', 'Cabbie's killer convicted of manslaughter', 'Jailed after four day rampage of violence'.

And so far I have read no further than page five. (To be fair, I must record that on page five there is some good news. The 205 bus, I learn, is now to run a 24-hour service.)

My years in Hackney witnessed the rise of inner-city gang culture. In all our big cities this culture is escalating. These gangs assault and rob and kill. Their members are always young, usually black, rarely female. Often the victim of a gang will be a member of another gang, someone who has trespassed as they see it on their own turf, sometimes a specific postcode. Others are frequently – and literally – caught up in the cross-fire. There are more such gangs in London than anywhere else in the country and more of them in Hackney than anywhere else in London. They include 'E9 Bang Bang', 'the Holly Street Boys', 'the Love of Money Crew', 'the Hoxton Boys', 'the Hackney Posse', 'the Well Street Boys' – there are at least a couple of dozen more known to the police. Many of these gangs are very highly organized, using the Internet to post intimidating footage on YouTube of their terrifying arsenals. Open any of their sites and there is a gun in your face. Some are simply loose associations of young people who have drifted into each other's company, but who are menacing enough so long as they hang about together. Many black teenagers in Hackney belong to a gang because they feel it is dangerous not to.

As a church we made little impact on Hackney's gang culture. First things first, we had to repair the roof.

Much of Hackney's crime is drug-related. Whoever is stealing the copper fittings from live gas meters is probably in need of the next fix. Much of the gun warfare is the conflict of cartels competing for greater control of the market in the drugs dispensed in the crack-houses and stinking stairwells on the borough's run-down estates. The fact that street prices for drugs are the lowest they have ever been only escalates that competition and the consequent violence.

What makes Hackney's violence so heartbreaking is that both its perpetrators and its victims are often little more than children. I wrote in my diary about Robert.

A small hill of flowers, a carpet of candles, a bar of Kit-Kat and a bottle of Lucozade mark the spot, not far from Hackney Town Hall, where sixteen-year-old Robert died, stabbed to death, allegedly by another schoolboy, on his way home from school. There are the poignant messages. 'Returned to God'. 'Rest in peace, our fallen soldier.' 'You can cry because he has gone, or you can do what he'd have done – smile, love, open your eyes, and go on.' It seems as if the knife that killed Robert has pierced the heart of our community more deeply than many another local murder. Hackney is crying 'Enough!'

A bitter footnote to this incident is that Robert was killed right outside a property belonging to our church, a house where once a jolly curate lived and merry children played ping-pong in the basement. For years the premises have been used by Hackney Council and for most of those years we have been trying to persuade Hackney to agree to a lease and a proper rent. (How else are we to mend the roof and pay the quota?) I am ashamed to think of the countless – and so far fruitless – hours we have spent trying to get the council to meet its obligations. There are, it now seems, other things we might have been doing.

There is some evidence that the level of violent crime in Hackney is dropping, though you would not think so from our local paper. The regular reports of knives being drawn or guns being fired become monotonous. Presumably that is why most such incidents are unreported by the national press. That said, we all heard about 'the Hackney Siege'.

'The Hackney Siege' was how the papers described it. The police encircled a property where a solitary gunman was holed out in a top-floor flat. Already it is slipping into history. Local residents, locked out of their homes for a fortnight, have moved back. Most businesses along the road have reopened, though not yet Elliston's Beauty Clinic, the premises immediately below the burned-out bed-sit in which the gunman barricaded himself. This is the place – or it was – for your 'facials', 'deep peel', 'nail extentions' (sic) and, if desperate, your 'body wraps'. Next door is 'Tony's Cafe' where I drop in for a mug of tea and a slice of cherry tart. I'm the only customer, for this is still a stretch of road where people prefer not to linger. Tony, who is Turkish, tells me how the police took over his flat upstairs. They drilled holes through his bedroom wall into the room next door where the gunman was staked out. Whether these holes were for the passage of CS gas, soup, intolerably loud music, or emollient messages isn't clear. Nor is it clear who is going to repair all the damage.

Those immediately affected by the siege suffered a wretched ordeal. But my impression is that the rest of Hackney was fairly nonchalant about it all. 'The Hackney Siege', including its tragic outcome, was waiting to happen. More people were annoyed by the re-routing of the No 38 bus along Dalston Lane than were surprised by someone taking potshots at policemen from an upstairs window.

The problem of inner-city violence is aggravated by the element of race. Street violence in our inner-cities is perceived – to use a term that has gained dangerous legitimacy – as 'black on black' crime.

If you come and see us – please do – avoid tea-time. Not because we're short of sandwich-spread but because approaching our Rectory as the kids spill out of school can be alarming. Warring gangs of teenagers congregate in the churchyard. Occasionally a tide of them will suddenly set off screaming through the tombs. It's the Gadarene demoniac joined by his mates. The 'bill' are doing their best. They have been given extra powers to 'stop and search'. 'They're harassing us. We're going to harass them,' a policeman assures me. So yesterday I return from my visits to find two white policemen frisking two black youths on my front drive. Today an expressionless schoolboy looks on as a young policewoman nervously inspects the knife she's found on him. An enormous constable writes the details in a tiny book. Our churchyard has become the stage where all the conflicting passions of our community are played out. The fury of black parents who claim that it's their children, rather than white kids, who are being targeted; the alarm that street-crime in Hackney, much of it 'kid on kid', is getting worse; the anger of the old who see children lost to all control;

the bitterness of the young who have ceased to hope – all this enacted on our consecrated ground. And in the midst of it all the huge hulk of Hackney Parish Church. No doubt a symbol of something.

Hackney's notoriety has made it the preferred location for fictional treatment of inner-city violence. Saul Dibb's film *Bullet Boy*, a powerful study of black Britain's gun culture, was shot in Hackney. Dreda Say Mitchell's superb debut novel *Running Hot* (Maia Press, 2004) perfectly captures the simmering feuds which periodically break to the surface in the exchanges of fire that take place on Hackney's streets. The dramas of 'murder mile' were brought to the stage in a play that enjoyed a successful run while I was in Hackney and about which I wrote in my diary.

'Close to a Bloodbath', 'Couple found in House of Horror', 'Babies in Shooting Hell', 'Turf-war Fear', 'Witch Girl in Torture Ordeal'. Those are the lurid headlines of the last five issues of the *Hackney Gazette*. They are windows on the world which is my home. Another such window is Kwame Kwei-Armah's brilliant play *Elminah's Kitchen*, now running at London's Garrick Theatre. *Elminah's Kitchen* is a Hackney café and the play explores the roots of the gang warfare which brings the gunfire to Hackney's streets. The *Hackney Gazette* is one of its props. A character is seen sitting at a table in the café – shortly before the shooting starts – turning its pages. But our local paper's headlines do not tell the whole of Hackney's story, otherwise few of us would choose to live here. Buried in the inner pages of the latest *Gazette* is a tiny piece offering another perspective on this troubled neighbourhood. The Council, we learn, wants us to recycle our aluminium. 'For every tonne of aluminium collected by Hackney Council, a tree will be planted here.' And I think of that tremendous text, 'And Abraham planted a tamarisk tree in Beersheba, and called there on the name of the Lord.' A daft thing to do in the desert. But whether in the wilderness of the Negev or in the wastelands of our inner-cities that in the end is the best we can do.

A parish priest in Hackney has to be streetwise. Moreover, if his home is his castle he has to make sure that – even if it lacks portcullis and drawbridge – it is at least well-secured. There is evidence that clergy are more liable than those in most other jobs to find themselves victims of violence. In my more Pauline moments I might have counted it a matter of indifference whether I lived or died. That was my privilege. But I could not allow my family to fall victim to such sentiments, however scriptural. So we made our house and garden as secure as we could. When a parishioner came to the rectory seeking ghostly counsel or, more often, a handout, he or she had to wait while innumerable bolts and keys were drawn and turned – and then the door remained chained until I was satisfied that it was safe to open it. Alas, it was a procedure that only imperfectly testified to the cordiality of the kingdom of God.

Sometimes the tide of Hackney's violence reached our rectory. Ahmed had a flourishing mobile phone business just up the road. He used to park his car on our front drive. Late one Saturday evening as he returned to his car two men followed him up our drive, knifed him in the leg, seized his takings, and made off. This was a couple of yards from our front door.

We became wary when we came home after dark. But wariness breeds suspicion and suspicion saps charity. One night our Rebecca, about ten at the time, warned us as we were about to get out of the car, 'There's a man over there.' Only when she pointed him out did I notice the dark figure crouched in the shadows by our garage. I wound down the window and asked him who he was. 'I'm homeless,' he said. Maybe he was homeless, but that didn't mean he didn't have a knife. Still in the car, I asked him to go. Which, slowly, sadly, he did. I heard him whisper as he went, 'I'm sorry. I'm sorry.' Sweet Jesus, it's not you who should have been sorry.

My diary records other incidents close to home.

Our front drive continues to serve as a rat-run for Hackney's villains. The other day, within an hour, two of them had sprinted up the drive, scrambled over the wall into our back garden, scaled the fence into the neighbouring property (a day-nursery, recently closed by a cash-strapped council and promptly done over by vandals), before escaping via next-door-but-one, the Hackney morgue. The second of these fleeing figures was hotly pursued by a little old man with a stick. The latter abandoned the chase outside our front door. There he still was, all in a lather, when I got to the door myself. 'I'll break his back!' he screamed. I asked, not very intelligently, whether I could be of any assistance. 'He's stalking my daughter,' he yelled. Then, dropping his voice, he added, 'He's a half-caste, you know.' What did I say? I forget. What could I have said? I've no idea. In Hackney it is often hard to say what is at once comprehensible, charitable, and true. So, as Wittgenstein concluded, 'Whereof I cannot speak, I'd better belt up about'.

Experience of petty crime fuels fear of worse. Three incidents in recent weeks make us nervous. Wally, who does odd jobs in our garden, was distressed to find that someone had climbed in and, very neatly, cut all the strings on a frame he'd lovingly made for our runner-beans. Then there's been the theft of our Burmese cat 'Parker'. Parker's teeth could do fearful damage as the mangled remains of the pigeons he dragged back into the rectory testified. There was something of Saki's *Sredni Vashtar* about him. I wouldn't be surprised if Parker returned one morning with bloody fragments in his maw, scraps of flesh torn from the hand that snatched him from us. And then someone tried to walk off with our Buddha. That serene presence in the corner of our garden, reminding us that 'all is emptiness, all is compassion', in fact weighs a ton and the thief did not get very far with it. Perhaps – 'just is the wheel, O horse-seller from the North' – he dropped it on his foot.

I am raking my Zen garden but not in a properly attentive and recollected frame of mind. Over the fence a fracas has erupted. Clearly there will be no peace within until there is some peace without so, with a curse that will not hasten my release from the wheel of rebirth,

I go to investigate. Outside our front door I find two Marks and Spencers security guards in conversation with a gentleman who they think has been shoplifting. They'd seen someone dash from the store – it's just across the road from us – and do a runner up our drive and they'd set off after him. Their suspicions are not unreasonable given that they have now found this man hiding under our car with a stash of M&S clothing stuffed in his anorak. The shoplifter offers no resistance. He is a desperately forlorn figure, a pathetic old man clearly in need of a square meal. The M&S heavies tell him that he's an effing unprintable and take him away. Later I learn that the store quickly established that he was a heroin addict and let him go.

Dusk falls softly on the Zen garden and all at last is still. But I am no longer at ease. I am troubled by the possibility that the wisdom of the Zen masters ('without support for feet or hands, sit only your buttocks') is not the answer to all of Hackney's problems.

The age is long past when there was a tacit understanding among villains that you did not steal things from a church. Across the years a number of items that were not nailed down 'disappeared'. Sometimes someone would help themselves from the collection. One Sunday a large family came to see their latest baby 'christened'. It was a happy enough service, though overshadowed by the fact that at the end one of the family walked off with the silver ewer we used to pour water in the font.

Crime in church is not just a problem for the police. It is a problem too for theologians. One Sunday I preached on the parable of the sheep and the goats. I said that we must be an inclusive church, undiscriminating in whom we welcome. A little later, while everyone gathered round the altar for communion, a woman dashed for the door. That's no big deal. In our church they came and went as the mood seized them. But this lady was clutching a handbag that was clearly not hers. Several in the congregation raced after her. After the service I pieced together what happened. Her pursuers caught up with her in a local side street. At which point she turned and drew a knife. Sensibly they backed off. The thief dropped the handbag – from which she'd taken a ten pound note – and fled. The police asked me whether we had CCTV cameras in our church. Perhaps by now they are installed. I recall pondering the contradictions of preaching and practice. Moments earlier I had asserted that Jesus comes to us in the person of the hungry and homeless. But supposing that Jesus then nicks your handbag?

Most of Hackney's violence, as in many more advantaged neighbourhoods, is hidden in the home. Signs of it are sometimes to be seen on the bruises children bring to school. I too, like many another priest, have wondered what to say on hearing from a tearful wife about what her respectable husband was doing to her. Sometimes such domestic violence was staged publicly.

A man and a woman are in conversation. She is clearly giving him a piece of her mind. He, a lumbering skinhead with a stud in his lower lip, is leaning on his bicycle. Suddenly she reaches out and smacks his face hard. He lifts his bicycle, swings it around his head and lunges towards her. She screams and heads off towards the nearby high-rise. Her bloke, if that is who he is, moves to follow her. But then he has second thoughts. He mounts his bike and rides off out of my life, if not, alas, out of hers.

Of course it is not only Hackney's poor who turn to crime or violence, nor is villainy anything new. In the eighteenth century, John Ward MP lived just round the corner from our rectory. As well as being a parliamentarian, Ward was a forger of banknotes. They caught up with him eventually and he was sent down for a long stretch. He was a pious prisoner. Like St Paul and John Bunyan, he made his cell his oratory. Among his papers this prayer was found: 'I beseech thee, O Lord, to preserve the two counties of Middlesex and Essex, and as I have a mortgage in Hertfordshire, I beg thee likewise to have an eye of compassion on that county.'

5

From the Ridiculous to the Sublime

I'm glad that our church is dedicated to a figure as accessible as John the Baptist. John the Baptist is someone you'd recognise in the street – unlike, say, the Holy Trinity. We had a memorable Patronal Festival in his honour this year. David Garlick, Vicar of Lewisham, preached a challenging sermon. He told us that if we had the bottle of the Baptist we too might end up in prison. The thought troubles me. A friend of mine has handled one of the heads of John the Baptist. (There are, I gather, several in competing reliquaries.) He says it looks like a desiccated grapefruit. I would not touch it myself, not from squeamishness but from fear that those shrivelled lips might whisper words I would not wish to hear. If ever there were a prophet who 'being dead yet speaketh' it is John the Baptist. How contemptuous he would be of the culture of today's Church of England! I picture him gate-crashing a meeting of the Archbishops' Council – 'the Sanhedrin' as some, disrespectful of their betters, now call it. Groping beneath his malodorous and verminous skins he extracts a couple of locusts from the colony nesting in his armpit and crams them into his mouth. His terrible eyes fix in turn on each at the table. 'Even now the axe is laid to the root of the trees,' he roars. Suddenly there is a rush for the door.

One of the ways in which the modern Church of England tries to keep up is by requiring clergy to undergo an annual 'ministerial review'. Most big businesses have similar procedures in place for their staff. The process requires the priest to reflect on his or her ministry over the previous twelve months and to identify ways in which that ministry might be made more effective. Priests are encouraged to make this assessment in the light of what they promised to be and to do when they were ordained and when they were put in charge of their parishes. To guide this self-scrutiny, a lengthy checklist of questions ministers might ask themselves is provided. Every minister is offered a 'consultant' who will look back with them over the past year and agree 'targets' for the coming year. The process is rounded off by a meeting with the bishop. Ten minutes later, so it feels, the carousel lurches into motion once more. Some clergy find this process helpful. Others find it irksome. A few, crushed by their sense of failure, are tempted to top themselves.

The intention of the ministerial review process is praiseworthy. As a priest, I am accountable. I am accountable to my conscience and my God, to my wife and my children, to my congregation and my bishop. The problem with the process is that it rests on two false premises. The first is the assumption that a parish priest can develop strategies and set targets in the way the chief executive of a secular organization does. The boss of Tescos has minions. He is the centurion who says 'Go' and, behold, someone goeth, 'Come' and someone cometh. I had no one in Hackney I could tell to come and go. The second premise is the fantasy that an incumbent of a short-staffed, cash-strapped parish, burdened with intractable buildings, *ex officio* obligations, and with all the unrealistic expectations made of him or her, is free to be the kind of priest that the ordinal envisages. I believe that I was called both to priesthood and to be a priest in Hackney, but there were many days when what in practice I had to do bore no relation to what I was ordained to do.

Like most incumbents of a historic parish, I was landed – literally 'landed' – with a raft of property. I remember a surveyor driving me round the back streets of Hackney soon after I arrived. He pointed out to me one insalubrious establishment after another. About each of them he had a single laconic comment – 'That's yours'. My confused impression at the time was of a succession of pool arcades, jellied-eel outlets, greasy spoons, and betting shops. But my most surreal memory of those early days is of a phone call from the leader of the Hackney Borough Council's gay and lesbian youth club. He thought I ought to know that a light

49

bulb had blown in the hall where they met. It appeared that I was the landlord. He couldn't replace the bulb because the council did not allow its operatives to climb ladders and what was I going to do about it? I forget what I said. Perhaps I defaulted to the evangel-icalism of my youth and promised to pray about it.

My *ex officio* role as a landlord led to some unpleasant corre-spondence. One Monday morning, getting off to a bright start, I received a summons to appear before the Bow Road Magistrates Court. The alleged offence was the non-payment of a 'non-domestic rate'. It appeared that, on one of the various properties of which I was landlord, someone – not me, m'lud – had been default-ing on the aforesaid rate. It was another case of 'when in doubt sue the Rector' and one more instance of being required, as the parish priest, to deal with a situation for which I had absolutely no aptitude, training, vocation, or inclination.

In the event I was spared a spell in Ford Open Prison, but having to contemplate the prospect of court proceedings brought home the contradictions of the situation I was in. I looked back wryly on the service at which I was instituted and inducted. It was a splendid occasion, rich in symbolism. I was led to the font, the pulpit, the altar; I received the keys and rang the bell; I promised to obey my bishop and I announced that the Ladies' Needling Group would in future meet on Tuesdays. But I ruefully reflected that one cere-mony had been omitted from the liturgy, the moment when the representatives of all the principalities and powers, temporal and spiritual, who have appointed a priest to his living, ascend a ladder and together empty a dustbin over his head.

As Rector of Hackney, I was trustee of several charities. For some of the duties of that role I was ill equipped. I confided my mis-givings to my diary.

One of the numerous charities of which I am a trustee is appointing a new fund manager. Their task will be to ensure that our assets are prudently and profitably invested. Quite right too. However, at our last meeting I was alarmed to learn that I was expected to be on the interviewing panel. Even on a sunny day I can't tell the difference between a busted convertible security and a price swap derivative. As it is my rule of life not to exercise myself in matters that are too high for me I tried to get off the hook. But my objections were overruled. Knowing my Saki if not my stock-market, I told the others at the table what my contribution to the selection process would be. 'I shall study their socks,' I said. 'One can always tell a good fund manager by his socks. These must command one's admiration without forfeiting one's respect.'

Among the duties incumbent on an incumbent that do not perceptibly advance the kingdom of God are those which pertain to the Annual Church Meetings. There are several of these meetings – the meeting that appoints the churchwardens is not competent to appoint the organizer of the Flower Rota, for example – and most parishes concertina the meetings into one session. The Rules which govern the conduct of these meetings are Byzantine. The only clergy who understand them are those who wear anoraks beneath their copes. Year by year I jollied everyone through these meetings and kept my irritation with the bureaucracy to myself – and to my diary.

What the Buddhists call 'right mindfulness' is required in my job. Currently I'm faced with the mountainous paperwork that goes with the Annual Church Meetings. Bumph about who has been elected to what has to go back to the Lord Warden of the Cinque Ports and the Akond of Swot. As usual, the Archdeacon's 'Articles of Enquiry', reminding me of the things I have left undone which I ought to have done, induce a crippling conviction of sin. This year members of the new Parochial Church Council are asked to declare their ethnic origin. (Black people on our PCC, who are the majority, are reluctant to do so. If this reluctance is general the final figures will be badly skewed.) Then there's a form headed 'Statistics for Mission', a title deserving this year's *palme d'or* for fatuous ecclesiastical slogans. In Holy Scripture dire judgement is reserved for those who yield to the

51

lust to count. I will alter my will in favour of the Archbishops' Council if they can tell me how all this number-crunching is going to advance the Kingdom of God here in Hackney.

Every seven years everything becomes yet more complicated. This is the Levitical seventh year when each parish has to shred its old electoral roll and draw up a new one. Everyone has to fill in Form SG1, 'Application for Enrolment on the Electoral Roll of the Parish'. Notes on the form tell you why it is so important to sign up. 'Joining the electoral roll,' it says, 'is an important statement of witness and a step along the path of discipleship.'

Soren Kierkegaard would not have regarded registering one's membership of the established church as an act of witness. He tells us what it means to be a witness. 'A witness to the truth is one who is scourged, maltreated, dragged from one prison to another and then at last crucified, or beheaded, or burnt, or roasted on a gridiron.' Let us not confuse matters. No doubt parishes should have up-to-date electoral rolls. But the costly *marturia* of Christian discipleship is something else entirely. Such, at least, are my sentiments which – sitting comfortably in my spacious study – I share with anyone interested.

The irony that measures intended to equip and encourage the clergy sometimes serve only to demoralize them was marvellously illustrated by one extraordinary communication which all the Hackney clergy received. I noted the gist of it in my diary.

Another week, another audit. This time it is a 'Clergy Skills Audit'. I'm asked by the suits at the Centre to indicate my 'level of experience to date' and to give a 'priority rating for future development' in no less than one hundred and twenty nine different areas of expertise 'which may be needed by all clergy'. I have to say, on a scale between one and five, how expert I am in fields as far-flung as 'Churchyards, D.A.C. and Faculties', 'Choreography of Worship' and 'Nuptial Masses'. Then I must rate between nought and ten how keen I am to bone up in each of these areas. I calculate that there are 55 to the power of 129 ways of completing this questionnaire. About the number of atoms in the universe. I am glad I was ordained long enough ago to have enjoyed a fulfilling ministry before the church capitulated to a culture which delights in such documents.

Once upon a time we managed without such 'managerialism'. But there are four less old-fogeyish objections to that survey. First, anyone with research experience, whether quantitative or qualitative, knows that such enquiries are never innocent. There is no such thing as an unloaded question. Questions are shaped by the agendas of those who ask them – and on this document those persons were not identified. Secondly, I was not told – and I would have liked to have known – who was to be made privy to this map which, had I chosen to supply it, would have charted the boundless Sahara of my ineptitude. Thirdly, many clergy already feel they are failures. A form that reminds them of one hundred and twenty nine areas in which they are supposed to be expert will only make the consolations of the bottle more tempting. Fourthly, the essence of Christian ministry is not in quantifiable skills, but in a kind of loving which cannot be calibrated. I thought again of the rector under whom I served my title, Canon Sandfield of Camborne. I'm sure he would have awarded himself a pitifully low score on such an 'audit'. Yet he was Christ to me and to all who knew him.

One of the benefits of good management, we are told, is that it guarantees greater 'transparency'. It is not clear to me, however, that the managerial measures put in place by the councils of the Church of England have achieved this transparency. My experience in Hackney was that much remains opaque.

An anxious lady, down to read a lesson, buttonholes me just as the service is about to start. She's in a state because she can't work out what she's supposed to read. Many round here are flummoxed by complicated paper-work. Books like the *Common Worship Lectionary*, with its baffling preface telling you what to do 'where Thomas is transferred from 3 July' and so on, terrify them. They scare me too. In solidarity with God's oppressed people, I have renewed my solemn vow never to find out what a 'proper' is or what on earth is meant by 'ordinary time'.

We are planning to start a monthly user-friendly 'family service', accessible to all ages. We wish this service to include the breaking of bread because we believe that if anything is for all the family it is the Eucharist, the sign and seal of our kinship in Christ. So far, so good. We then run up against the fact that we are obliged to use words – dear Lord, so many words – which are user-hostile. The authorised Eucharistic prayers are the biggest problem. They say too much and they say it for too long. We have known that from the first day we used them. What troubles me more, riffling through the collected works of Michel Foucault, is that those prayers are prime examples of what he has taught us to see in so many texts of our time, the danger-ous collusion of knowledge, language and power. Much in post-modernism is half-baked, if not downright gobbledy-gook. But this much at least we have learned from its gurus – that texts by those who know, in the language of those who know, are instruments of control and coercion. Sometimes on Sundays, as I obediently say what I am supposed to say, I think that I hear a great cry (not permitted by General Synod) 'Let my people go!'

For much of my time in Hackney I was entrusted with a curate. I tried my best to safeguard him from the often giddily inconsequen-tial matters that came my way as rector and to leave him free to get on with what he was called to do. I paid tribute to him in my diary.

Someone warned our new curate that his doings might be reported in this diary. He has nothing to fear. Jonathan is what the Prayer Book says he should be – 'grave, not double-tongued, not given to much wine, not greedy of filthy lucre'. He is doing what the Prayer Book says he should – 'instructing the youth in the Catechism, searching for the sick, poor, and impotent people of the parish' and the rest. Like holy matrimony, to be a curate is an honourable estate instituted by God. There is something very Christian in the fact that the higher you are promoted in the Church of England the harder it is to do any good. Our curate spends his time in pastoral care and evangelistic outreach, in the study of Holy Scripture and works of devotion, in teaching little children and in comforting the aged and infirm. Meanwhile I worry about the fungus growing on the church wall and struggle with a petition for a Faculty to renew the tarmac over where we used to bury our suicides. I have no idea what Bishops and Archbishops do, but I suspect that they are even more preoccupied with the penultimate.

Eventually I was told that we were not to get another curate. I gathered that I had been struck off the register of 'training incumbents'. I was sad about this, sorry for myself, but sorry too that some devout and learned deacon was to be denied the chance to test their metal in the heart of Hackney. The news that from that day onwards I was to be on my own prompted an extended entry in my diary. I wrote in acid.

Today's tasks typify the inner-city ministry for which a thorough theological education is indispensable. The post and emails take a couple of hours. There is the regular mailing from the centre, full of flyers and attachments about forthcoming attractions. Not all of these are for the diary. A tactful reply is needed to a resident of one of our almshouses who complains that her neighbour has abandoned a malodorous carpet near her front door. There's a letter concerning the controversial closure of the Council day nursery occupying a site which was once the end of our garden. This is a can of worms and volley of letters in different directions is needed to keep the lid on it.

A notice about the rent review of another of our innumerable properties is quite beyond me. So far as I understand it the tenants are objecting that the building has no access to the outside world. Presumably they are not Cistercians of the Strict Obedience. I leave to last a stern warning that we have seven days to pay the water rate for another parsonage in the parish before they send round the heavies. Eventually I get out of the house – only to discover that they're digging a trench through the churchyard. A fat purple pipe is being

55

laid the length of it. A genial workman tells me that it's all to do with the CCTV cameras they're installing. That's the first I've heard about it. Certainly we want fewer muggings among our tombs, but the dead too have a right not to be disturbed and I'm quickly back on the phone to find out about injunctions. Now one of my church-wardens drops in. We discuss what to do about the lethal asbestos cladding around the church boiler and the installation of vents in our pongy kitchen. The next meeting is with a man come to inspect the rectory garden wall, a length of which is about to collapse. Then it's time for a chat with our treasurer about next year's huge hike in the quota.

So the day unfolds. And no curate to help. Surely it is to the loss of someone with a trained theological mind that he or she has been forbidden the opportunity to apply that mind to such challenges.

The stress which most inner-city clergy experience, and which some own up to, is not simply a consequence of overwork. (Sufficient evidence of the church's triumphal entry into cuckoo-land is provided by the fact that clerical stress has now been solemnly calibrated by an instrument known as 'the Maslach Burnout Inventory'.) Conscientious clergy are burdened more by the contradictions of their work than by its volume. There are different orders of tiredness. There is the tiredness that comes at the end of a day well spent, the kind of exhaustion that a whisky and a good night's sleep will swiftly repair. But there is a different order of tiredness, a weariness of spirit which deepens every day. This is the exhaustion, perilously close to despair, which overtakes many ministers in contemplating the gulf between the vision which once beckoned them to ministry and the prospect of what actually has to be done.

In recent years innumerable younger clergy, faced by this conflict between what they aspired to be and what they have to be, have cut and run. They have not left it too late to start again. They have retrained as teachers, health-workers, lawyers, supermarket shelf-stackers, or whatever.

I was too old and too dim to start a new career. Anyway I never wished to, at least not for long. Despite everything, Hackney was far too much fun. There was, too, a theological reason for staying put. I kept going because of what I believed and because I found what I believed vindicated in experience. The faith that sustained me was the Christian claim that 'the Word was made flesh' and the conviction that what we call the Incarnation was not only an event in history but that it is also an abiding principle. The Word was made flesh – *flesh* of all absurd and unlovely substances. The sublime was revealed in the ridiculous. That was the once-and-for-all *event* of the Incarnation. But the sublime still is – present tense – revealed in the ridiculous. That is the *principle* of the Incarnation. Of all human avocations there are none more dotty than that of a parson. From Victorian copies of *Punch* to the *Vicar of Dibley*, clergy have always been recognized as comic. But sometimes the ludicrous is transfigured. It happened that once in Palestine. It happens still in inner-city parishes. It happened in my time in Hackney when, now and again and in a way I could not begin to explain, the loopy was somehow bathed in a greater light. I noted of some of those occasions in my diary.

I visit an ancient of days lately discharged from hospital. She is seething with indignation. Her complaint is against, first, 'the slip of a girl', who confiscated her senna-pods and who sent her to bed at half-past-seven, and, secondly, the God who has returned her for no apparent reason to a life drained of purpose. I can do nothing to recover the sequestrated senna-pods but I can assure her that she is someone needed and needed now. My first grandchild is about to be born and I require immediate advice on how to be a grand-parent. She has plenty of that to give and, fortified by the can of Guinness at her elbow, she lets me have it. Her theology of childhood is that of the book of Proverbs – 'Iniquity is bound up in the heart of a child but the cane will thrash it out of him'. Clearly she would endorse George Whitfield's high Calvinist view of 'the merit of breaking a child's will betimes'. The opportunity to deliver herself of these opinions cheers her up enormously. I reflected that it had been a successful pastoral visit, even if someone of her integrity should probably seek alternative episcopal oversight.

'Aaaaargh! . . . .' The explosion of sound, like the cry from the Centre Court at Wimbledon of someone propelling a tennis ball at a hundred miles an hour, rings across our garden. Our guests, as we sit by the pond taking tea, are discomposed. We reassure them. Overlooking our rectory garden, above the back of a shop, is a small hall housing one of Hackney's many martial arts schools. The sound you hear is the noise you must make as you leap four feet in the air and kick out to within an inch of your opponent's neck. I see here the possibility, cassock-alb permitting, of offering something more stimulating than a limp handshake to departing members of the congregation.

I receive a note from one of my churchwardens to say that she has been approached by a Japanese lady who is writing a book about church toilets. Would I meet this lady on Sunday before the service to show her our facilities? In the event she is late and I'm already robed and ready to announce the first hymn. But she is both charming and insistent and she persuades me to delay proceedings while she takes a series of carefully composed photographs of me – in full fig – standing at the open door of our amenity for the disabled. There is no time to ascertain from her whether she is working on a scholarly article for a learned journal, on something glossier for the coffee table, or – a possibility too appalling to contemplate – on an illustrated text to meet certain minority interests. Fortunately few of my congregation are likely to be scanning the top shelves of the seedier Tokyo newsagents.

Someone has marked the place in the Bible in the rector's stall, not as they should with a ribbon of seasonal colour or a card with a comforting text, but with a slip from a doctor's notepad. I am distracted, while conducting the annual service for the Londinium Grand Lodge (Western Hemisphere District) of the Independent United Order of Mechanics by 'Today's Rheumatology Reminder'. 'Traditionally,' I read, 'osteoarthritis is regarded as inexorably progressive. However recent research has shown that it may be arrested or even reversed in animals'. While I digest this pleasing information there falls a great silence and I realise that I have failed to announce the next hymn – 'Oh Mechanics, we are travelling' (to the tune of 'John Brown's Body').

A note is pressed into my hand at the church door. 'Dear Father. This is a message from the Lord. The Lord says people who suffer from AIDS should drink from the green-skin water-coconut. The good Lord says it will cure some but it won't cure all.' I am pleased that the lady who shared this disclosure with me feels at home in our church – just as I'm glad that a highly qualified young woman doctor working with AIDS victims has also chosen to worship with us. 'All one' and all that. Despite our different views about God and coconuts.

On some events, however, heaven's light does not shine.

I am an educated adult. I am in a public place. I am wearing an outfit thought fetching in Pisidian Antioch in the fourth century. I am holding in my hands what appears to be a model of the first man-made satellite to orbit the earth, placed in space by the Russians in 1957. I am singing the following words 'The Christingle is made of an orange.' And nobody is laughing.

A priest's role in the inner-city is a walk-on part in a comedy. But it is the divine comedy. There are moments in inner-city ministry – they are very precious – when the touch of eternity is palpable. Such moments take us by surprise.

Sometimes a baptism would be such an occasion, the 'means of grace' suddenly becoming a 'moment of grace'. I think of Leroy's 'christening', as of course they all called it. Most of Leroy's huge extended family, I imagine, had not been inside a church for years. They were at a loss about how to behave. They masked their nervousness and uncertainty by talking louder than necessary and by laughing for no obvious reason. There were several video cameras. East Enders love these gizmos and I had long ago abandoned the struggle to control their use in church. I got everyone to sit down. I told them that Jesus loves Leroy and that we were welcoming him into God's family. I told them that you don't have to be big enough or old enough or good enough or clever enough to belong to that family. I told them that little Leroy mattered to God as much as the whole wide world put together. When it came to the baptism itself I sloshed lots of water over Leroy. He howled – and I suggested that his howls were Leroy's 'Amen' to what we had done. Suddenly I was overwhelmed by the weight of what was happening. Two millennia fell away and we were in Galilee again. I heard someone say, 'Whoever receives one such child receives me.' I looked around. Leroy's family and friends were now as focused as at the start they had been distracted. I wondered whether I dared tell them who, for us, this child was.

Campaigns to recruit more clergy make much of the privilege and pastoral opportunities the parson enjoys in so often sharing the most important times of a family's life, when a child is born, when a couple marries, or when someone dies. That's what clergy do, it's supposed. They baptize babies; they marry people; they bury the dead. In fact the numbers of baptisms, weddings and funerals in church is in steep decline. At St John-at-Hackney we still had some baptisms – Leroy was not alone. There was the occasional funeral – more of those in a moment. But church weddings had virtually ceased. In my last four years as rector we had one church wedding. It was a memorable occasion both for its rarity and because the bride arrived at church an hour and a half late.

Not so long ago it was all very different. I treasure a letter from Michael Hocking who in the 1930s was a curate at St John-at-Hackney. This is what he tells me:

'There were weddings every Saturday, fifteen or sixteen I think. We never prepared people. Anybody who could convince the parish clerk that they were entitled to get married was signed on. We never saw any of them before or after. Nearly all the brides were pregnant, some very pregnant, but always in white. The bridegroom had to walk up the aisle unaided (many were drunk). Fortunately there was a cold water tap in the north porch and often the bridegroom's head was held under it.'

Now that tap has gone and so too have the weddings. Should I point out to those agonizing over the Church of England's policy on marriage that – in Hackney at least – no one is much interested?

The Church of England certainly still supposes that most couples planning to get married want a church wedding. I commented in my diary on a remarkable publication I received that reflected this endearing misapprehension.

'Experience a touch of elegance with Le Meridien Hotels.' 'Visit our flagship store in Mayfair and you'll find a beautiful range of jewellery in silver, gold and platinum.' 'Posh Parties & Do's for the *creme de la creme* services of wedding coordinators.' 'Honeymoon in Vegas.' And so on for page after silken page. Spend, spend, spend! Buy yourself the perfect wedding! The gems I quote are from a glossy magazine which has landed, unsolicited, on my door-mat and which I am invited to give to couples planning to wed. Bride and groom wanting the best for their big day are peculiarly vulnerable to this kind of predatory advertising. If they are well-heeled they can afford to fall for it. But if they are poor and are duped – and it is the poor of parishes like mine who are most vulnerable to such exploitation – they may well find that they have begun their marriage deep in debt. Such a publication marinates marriage in the spirituality of the market-place. It reeks of mammon. But what else are we to expect from a secular marketing organisation? Except that it is not produced by a secular marketing organisation but by the Diocese of London to be 'distributed by the Clergy in the Churches within the Diocese'. (For the record there are one hundred and fifty white faces pictured in its pages and four black.)

I was sad that we had so few church weddings. My experience of the secular alternatives makes me feel that with their passing much is being lost. Sutton House is a National Trust property in the parish of St John-at-Hackney. It is the nearest thing that the East End has to a stately home. Like lots of these posh places it is now a popular venue for weddings. Sutton House has fifty, sixty, seventy weddings a year – ten times as many weddings as we had in St John's Church. I am told that there are some pretty little country churches which still have lots of weddings. But it is a case of 'Hackney today, Nether Wallop tomorrow' and very soon church weddings will be a thing of the past. So be it.

What I do find alarming however are the constraints placed on a couple wanting to wed in some ducal des-res. We had a family wedding recently in the swanky surroundings of Osterley House. Bride and groom asked me to say a short prayer at the ceremony. This I was forbidden to do. The legislation is absolutely draconian. Nothing that could be construed as religious was permitted. No prayers, no 'religious music' (whatever that is), no religious sign or symbol. If you so much as crossed your legs an apparatchik would have flung you out. It was totally Stalinist. Some pressure group must have lobbied for the law to be drafted in this way, a law which denies couples – just because they want a gracious setting for their big day – even a token prayer for God's blessing on their marriage. I await reassurance that it was not the church, seeing its influence drain away, being spiteful.

Thank God, the parish priest does still sometimes share times of family joy and sorrow. Sometimes the strands of joy and the sorrow are strangely interwoven.

I sit at a bedside where a mother is dying. With me is her daughter who is holding her mother's hand and singing gently. The daughter's voice is quiet, serene, and extraordinarily beautiful. 'Jesus knows about my struggle. He will guide me till the day is done. There is no friend like the friend in Jesus. No, not one. No, not one.' We are in a ward at the Homerton Hospital. Tonight this is none other but the house of God and the gate of heaven.

There are far fewer church funerals than there used to be, at least in the East End. The undertaking industry is driven by commercial priorities. It suits the books of the funeral director if the obsequies take place at the crematorium or cemetery without time-consuming ceremonies in church. It also helps the undertaker to have a list of compliant hedge-priests with empty diaries who can be relied on – for the usual consideration in cash – to do the honours at the crematorium or the grave at whatever time suits the undertaker.

Nevertheless just occasionally I found myself taking a funeral service. In church or at the graveside, I often felt the touch of the transcendent. I shall end this chapter with some memories of these occasions. These were the times – however sad they were – when I was in no doubt that I was where a priest is supposed to be.

Someone's making a killing burying Hackney's dead but it's not me. Quite who the rogues are who've cornered all the funerals round here no one seems to know. So it was a big surprise to be asked to take Barbara's. Barbara never went to church but she was clearly a saint. She had been married nearly sixty years and had been the matriarch of a huge extended family of East Enders all of whom adored her. I did my best for them and they took me to their heart. I was overwhelmed by their gratitude for a funeral service in which I simply tried to be true to her memory and true to the gospel. We sang the songs Barbara sang in the pub and we sang 'Praise my soul the King of Heaven'. I said in my sermon that the love she had for them and they for her had its source in the love that hung the sun and all the stars. My fleeting involvement with this family was a poignant reminder of the time when this was what parish ministry was all about.

A funeral at Manor Park Cemetery. I am there far too early and I decide to go for a short walk. I love meandering through cemeteries and churchyards. Nowhere else are the mind's storms so swiftly stilled. Somewhere far across the other side of the cemetery a Caribbean funeral is taking place. Around the grave they are singing the lovely old Gospel songs, 'Yes, we'll gather at the river' and the rest. The singing is punctuated by the ringing 'Alleluias' of those who know that the grave has no victory. The funeral I have to take is a more melancholy business. All my attempts to contact the family have come to nothing and, beyond a name, I do not know who it is I am burying or who these people are who are bidding their perfunctory farewells. The grave is a stone's throw from the railway and I have to raise my voice above the clatter of passing trains. Not that anyone is listening. No one is disrespectful but equally no one appears to perceive that something important is happening. And no one, I fear, is transported by the beauty of the words of the Prayer Book service, any more than were the compilers of our modern orders of service else they would not have so horribly undone them.

It only takes a good funeral for my finely-spun post-modernism to unravel. I reason that religion has a job to do, that what is all-important is its task, not the correspondence to reality of its metaphysical claims. What matters are not religious 'truths' beyond verification or falsification, but religion's inalienable role. I am as content as a Cupitt that religious language evokes, inspires, and admonishes, but that it neither refers nor describes. Until, that is, I come to conduct Eileen's funeral when my clever-dick non-realism collapses like a house of cards. Eileen was a mischievous Caribbean child whose vivacity did not fade when as a young woman she settled on our shores. And she was a wonderful Christian. At her funeral her brother sang a solo. Quietly, wistfully, plaintively he sang, 'There's a land beyond the river, that we call the sweet forever . . .' When he came to the refrain his voice was little more than a whisper.

> *'Don't you hear the bells now ringing,*
> *Don't you hear the angels singing?*
> *It is the glory hallelujah jubilee.*
> *In the far off sweet forever, just beyond the shining river,*
> *Where they ring the golden bells for you or me'*

'In the far off sweet forever, just beyond the shining river . . .' Eleven words which would never be admitted to a modern hymnal, still less to *Common Worship*, yet whose artless eloquence is such that it's a struggle to stay sufficiently composed to carry on with the service. Does such language do no more than voice a disposition to look forward, a resolve to live optimistically? Or does it speak of what one day will truly be? I am no longer so sure and my uncertainty leaves me exposed to awful possibilities which in my mind I had long abandoned. Dear Lord, I do just pray that when my head stops spinning it will still be facing the front.

Vincent came to this country from Antigua in the 1950s. He was a lovely man with a great sense of fun and he must have enjoyed his funeral. There was a crowd of his mates outside on the porch as the cortège arrived. At which point large flakes of plaster from the decomposing portico began to flutter down among them. People in posh churches would have tut-tutted and written to the Bishop. Vincent's friends dissolved in gales of laughter. There was, too, a pleasing misprint in the order of service. That old tear-jerker 'Now the labourer's task has done' refers to the 'farther shore' where 'the work of life is tried by a juster judge than here'. On the service sheets 'juster judge' appeared as 'jester judge'. 'Jester judge'. I like that. Perhaps, when the divine comedy is done, the words we'll wake up to will be 'I was only joking'.

6

'The Ugliest Building in Christendom Bar One'

Today I noticed an elderly man struggling to dislodge a huge stone from the coping of our churchyard wall. Eventually he succeeded in shifting it. I watched him stagger up the steps of the porch and, with a huge effort, hurl it at the locked door of our church. Then he stumbled away before I could catch him. Back at the Rectory, I told the family what I'd seen. We wondered who this poor chap was and what was his problem. Was he perhaps in poor mental health? Was he drunk? Was he both? I ventured an alternative hypothesis. I suggested that he was probably a retired clergyman and of entirely sound and sober mind. I surmised that he had served faithfully in a series of benefices, each one blessed by a splendid church building for which he had been responsible. I speculated further that each of these proud buildings had proved inimical to the mission he had believed himself called to fulfil. I suggested that the burden of these buildings had at last broken his spirit. Now, several times a week, he was taking the train from his home for retired clergy and was picking off the churches of his former diocese one by one. Before each great door, like a latter-day Ezekiel, he was performing an act of 'prophetic symbolism', invoking the judgement of the Lord on a community which, called to live in tents, had preferred to build itself temples. Merry laughter rang round the Rectory. They thought I was joking.

A few days after those words appeared in the *Church Times* I received a distressing letter from the wife of a retired clergyman. She told me that she recognized her husband in the old man I had described. She said that in his time he had been the incumbent of a number of parishes, in each of which he had been saddled with an intractable building. These buildings, she told me, proved the shipwreck of his ministry. His wife grieved for a good priest who, forced wherever he went to put plant above people, finally lost all heart and was left a broken man.

I did not allow our building to undo me to that extent. But I recognize that it came perilously close to doing so.

For centuries Hackney was served by a splendid medieval parish church. Towards the end of the eighteenth century, however, they decided to pull it down and to build something greater. (A man in the Bible did much the same with his barns and we know what happened to him.) Local historians tell us that the reason for demolishing the old church and erecting a much bigger one was that the old building was too small for Hackney's growing population. Certainly many wealthy families moved into Hackney, building their fine houses, in the eighteenth century. Lots of schools too were started in Hackney at that period and it was something of a squash when their pupils were trooped into church.

Too many bums, too few pews. I concede the truth, so far as it goes, of this explanation of why Hackney's old church, save for its ancient tower, was razed to the ground in the 1790s and the present church of St John-at-Hackney built as its replacement. But that is not the whole story. As we have seen, during the eighteenth century Hackney had become a centre of nonconformity. Numerous dissenting congregations had built their own chapels in the parish. In 1786 the Calvinists had started their college in Homerton. (The college survives – though John Calvin no longer has any say in its governance – as Homerton College, Cambridge.) The established church in Hackney was alarmed by this rapid growth of dissent in the parish. They saw it as a threat. The establishment's response was to build a church of such a size that no one would be left in any doubt as to who was in charge. The new church, while certainly providing the extra seats needed, asserted by its sheer scale the power of the establishment over those who dared question its authority. Buildings say things. The statement made by the church consecrated on 15 July 1797, the church which gave me such headaches two hundred years later, was that the Church of England by law established was far stronger than any impertinent conventicle that had the temerity to challenge it.

The church of St John-at-Hackney – the building, not the people – remains a monument to establishment power and establishment arrogance. The power has long since drained away and perhaps slowly we are learning a little humility, but the monument, like the broken trunk of Ozymandias in the desert, remains. And – Lord, have mercy upon them – the rector, churchwardens and PCC are expected to maintain it.

That said, the first time I commented in my diary about our building, soon after my arrival in Hackney, I was relatively upbeat about it.

> Our booklet about the church quotes George MacDonald's observation that St John-at-Hackney is 'the ugliest church in Christendom, bar one'. I'd love to know which he thought the ugliest. I'm also distressed by his comment. I have always treated MacDonald's lightest remark as a word from Sinai and I hate to disagree with him. George MacDonald certainly had a problem about churches. He found them spooky places, architecturally and theologically short of sunshine. His aversion to them went back to the church of his childhood, a chilling tabernacle that bred bad doctrine like some foul fungus that only spawns in the dark. Certainly ours is a big church. It would be ideal for all-weather hang-gliding. But local people love it and I see why. It is a sublime space. Crowded communities need indoor spaces as well as outdoor ones. One of my jobs will be to protect that space, currently threatened by pianos. Recently there were eight in the church. We are now down to five but we could afford to shed two or three more. I know someone who knows someone who makes reproduction medieval siege-engines as a hobby. Apparently old pianos make ideal ammunition. I must get hold of his phone number.

'The ugliest building bar one,' said George MacDonald. In fact those were not his exact words. During my Hackney years I reread everything MacDonald wrote and eventually I tracked down the source of his comment. What MacDonald actually said allows us to locate a little more closely the whereabouts of the church he regarded as Christendom's ugliest and, more importantly, the reason why he objected so strongly to a church he regarded as only marginally less hideous.

MacDonald's novel *Guild Court*, first published in 1867, is the story of a prodigal son. MacDonald's wayward hero eventually comes to his senses and sets off home. The last few miles of his journey are through Hackney. The tower, all that is left of the old church, tells him that he does not have far to go.

> He saw the grey time-worn tower of the old church of Hackney, now solitary, its ancient nave and chancel having vanished, leaving it to follow at its leisure, wearied with disgust at the church which has taken its place and is probably the ugliest building in Christendom, except the parish church of a certain little town in the north of Aberdeenshire.[5]

So we are a little nearer to knowing what, for MacDonald, was the ugliest building of them all. More important, the context of his comments explains why it was that he so loathed the building that loomed over my rectory and my life. MacDonald was always clear whose side he was on in the immemorial warfare between institutionalized religion and the way of Jesus. In the story of the prodigal son, which inspired *Guild Court* and which with different characters MacDonald repeatedly retold in his many novels, the son is welcomed back – not to a church, nor to a religious institution – but to his father's home and his father's heart. MacDonald judged churches, not only their ministers and congregations but also their buildings, by how faithfully they expressed God's inexorable, unconditional, and non-condemnatory love. By this one criterion MacDonald judged the building, whose keys I was given at my induction, and found it wanting. Church buildings say things and not just about the people who build them. They talk about God too. MacDonald believed that what the structure of St John-at-

Hackney says about God – that he is a high, haughty, cold, and forbidding deity – is not true. Even the best friends of St John's could not claim that it is a homely building. Thank God, those who worship there are much more hospitable.

Looking back on my years as Rector of St John-at-Hackney, I recognize how the vast bulk of our building, with its multiple and insatiable demands, increasingly bore down on my back and threatened to break it. The building was above all a cancer on my conscience. How could we justify preserving a building seating two thousand for a congregation of sixty or seventy? Sometimes I would lay awake at night in a cold sweat and hot rage that, in one of the poorest neighbourhoods of Europe, we were contemplating spending hundreds upon hundreds of thousands upon thousands of pounds on a structure ideally suited for the assembly of airships. The rousing rhetoric was that our building was a great and glorious asset and that we should seek to maximize its potential as a resource for our mission and our service to the community. The truth was otherwise. As is the case for countless other churches up and down the land, the fabric of our building dictated our agenda, drained our budget, and exhausted our energies for one reason only. Like Everest, it was there.

Sensing the onset of paranoia, I consulted my spiritual director. He gave me a simple mantra to repeat, 'Bugger the building.' Alas, the burden still didn't roll away, as my diary reminds me.

When curates exceed their station the consequences can be costly. Take our church. (Someone please do.) With much junketing we have just been celebrating the bicentenary of its consecration. It was, as I say, all the curate's fault. The rector of the day ('a little puny consumptative man') was never there. During one of his protracted absences the curate had the bright idea of demolishing the old church and building a new one. A nicer class of person was moving into Hackney. More space was needed both for bottoms and carriages. A building was needed big enough to permit the worship of Almighty God at a sanitary distance from one's domestics. Such were the arguments. All eyewash, of course, as a brave minority at the time pointed out. The immense edifice the curate had built was, and is, an assertion of the might of the establishment. Dissenting chapels and academies were springing up all around the parish. Here was proof that the Church of England could have them all for breakfast. Not that the curate was the first to build a temple for which posterity had to pay the price. As the Archdeacon of Hackney pointed out, in a sermon to puncture the bicentenary balloons around the pulpit, that distinction belongs to Solomon – Solomon who, contemplating the full enormity of what he had done, pleaded to be forgiven.

I had inherited a church only slightly smaller than the Albert Hall. Blotches of damp soiled the false ceiling beneath the leaking roof But it was not only 'the waters above the firmament' we had to fight. 'The waters under the firmament' threatened to engulf us. One morning I went across to the church to find that our senile, refractory, hideously expensive, and virtually useless heating system had burst its bowels and fell fluids were welling up through our floorboards. To contain these problems, merely to renovate the existing fabric and to install functional heating, a sum with a cascade of noughts would have been needed. 'There's always the lottery,' they told me. But in Hackney it is the very poor who buy lottery tickets. I was not opposed to a flutter, but even my sluggish conscience protested at paying for a swanky church out of the wreckage of their dreams. Again I was dogged by that simple question – what would we do if we believed that Christianity were true?

My conscience made its protest, but not very powerfully. We applied for a lottery grant – and those who have travelled that road will testify to how protracted and exhausting an exercise that is. The hundred thousand awarded was just enough to patch up one corner of our porous roof. We ourselves paid for the buckets and mops that we had to get out again a week or two later as once more the rains came down and the rains came through.

It was reassuring to be occasionally reminded that my problems with our building were not some private paranoia.

I was asked to take Bill's funeral. Sixty years ago Bill had been a server at the church of St Mary of Eton, Hackney Wick. Sitting in the back pew of the crematorium chapel was an old priest. It was Father Augustine Hoey who all those years ago had been a curate at St Mary's. He had prepared Bill for confirmation and now, a lifetime later, he was there to say good-bye to him. Father Hoey went from Hackney to join the Community of the Resurrection, where he was a novice with Trevor Huddleston. Today he is a Roman Catholic and a Benedictine Oblate. I chatted with this dear and saintly man after the service. I told him that I was the minister at St John-at-Hackney. His face lit up with one of those radiant smiles that illuminate the faces of those who walk with God. 'Such an ugly church,' he said.

The half-way point of my incumbency coincided with the turn of the millennium. By then the scale of the damage being done by our building to our life, our mission, and our worship was becoming all too clear. An evening at the theatre and renewed exposure to *King Lear* – the greatest work in English literature, not excluding the King James Bible – illuminated our situation.

Light is shed on our woes by the current RSC production of *King Lear*. (Nigel Hawthorne, despite the scathing comments of critics who think you can't do Lear unless you shout, is superb.) Lear and the weird bunch of odd-balls and misfits with him in the wilderness – no roof over their heads, not even a leaky one – are a community of the redeemed. Our salvation too is only possible 'outside the gate' where the only shelter is beneath a gibbet on a little hill.

My millennial dream is of the church flogging all its impossible buildings and giving the money to OXFAM, of the bishops burning their daft hats on a bonfire of our baffling new lectionaries, of our ceasing to bicker about metaphysical minutiae beyond verification or falsification, of the General Synod voting for its own extinction, and of all of us wandering out on to some sufficiently blasted heath – the Hackney Marshes would do nicely – and starting again.

Then one day a large lump of masonry fell from the cornice of the church. There was the fear that more masonry might descend, necessitating the distribution of hard hats with the hymn books. The threat to our heads concentrated our minds. It was Whitsun and the Hackney clergy chapter was discussing the future of the church in London. I made my millennial suggestion. 'Meet up on Hackney Marshes and begin again.' And I added, Pentecost being upon us, 'Or an upper room would do'.

In the event we did not relocate on Hackney Marshes or find that upper room. We did what every organization with a problem does. We hired a consultant. We appointed Hannah, a theologian who believed that even the most stubbornly recalcitrant pile of bricks can be conscripted to the cause of the kingdom. What Hannah helped us to envision was not a conservation of the existing building, nor a conservative reordering of it, but a radical redevelopment of it. The new St John-at-Hackney would have at its centre a sacred space, a beating heart of prayer and worship. That was never in question. As for the rest of the building, in partnership with others we would look for ways to redeem its vacant spaces, including its cavernous stairwells and an area as big as an aircraft hanger above the ceiling and beneath the roof, so that our church might at last become a *parish* church in more than name.

The one certainty about our building was that in future we would have to share it. Possibly with a multiplex cinema, a sushi restaurant, a salsa dance school, several lush penthouses, a contemporary art studio (where goats with heads at each end would be pickled), and an organic mushroom farm. I cherished the hope that there would still be room for the hang-gliding.

The hang-gliding – and the bells. Whatever had to be done to our colossus of a church, I trusted that its bells would not fall silent.

The church of St John-at-Hackney is surmounted by a tower which baffled Nikolaus Pevsner. ('Only St Anne Soho is comparable in oddity'.) The glory of our tower is less in what you see of it than in what you hear from it, a peal of bells of incomparable splendour. My prayer is that when one day soon our church is turned into a multi-storey car-park they'll at least keep the bells. I have always loved church bells and admired bell-ringers. I've never had any sympathy for clergy who bellyache because their bell-ringers don't stay on for the church service. For the late Queen Mother our tower rang 'a half-muffled peal of 5040 Plain Bob Triples' and for the Queen's Golden Jubilee '5040 Grandsire Triples'. ('Plain Bob Triples' 'Grandsire Triples' – the very words are bells.) Last Sunday I dedicated the two peal boards recording these signal achievements. 'Bells, more than stars, are our fate,' wrote Ronnie Knox, 'and our little life is rounded with their pealing.' Though I am no bell-ringer, I feel a great affection for our bells, indeed a certain kinship with them. After my years in Hackney I too need my clappers rebushed.

Hannah, our consultant, was a wise counsellor. She was adamant that any scheme for the redevelopment of our building should take into account the needs of the wider community and the wider church. Thus a lengthy and detailed process of consultation was launched. Hannah made it clear that the project must be anchored in a biblical understanding of the mission of the church as the people of God. She sent us back to our Scriptures to study the role of sacred places in the divine economy. And she insisted that, because this redevelopment was to happen in Hackney and not half way up the garden path to heaven, it must be properly costed and budgeted.

We were fortunate at that point in our history in having on our PCC a nucleus of exceptionally able people, including some with considerable experience of major redevelopment projects. Some years previously one of our team had sorted out London Zoo with its umpteen listed buildings, including its Grade 1 listed penguin pool. As important as their expertise was their commitment to the Christian cause and to Christian priorities. We felt that we had caught a tide and that now was the time, the *kairos* moment, the God-given opportunity to make our building, which for so long had impeded our mission, a means of grace for a new millennium.

The diocese did not see it this way. Risk-averse, they urged caution. I was within a year or two of retirement and I was warned not to embark on a big scheme that would 'tie the hands of my successor'. The sound from the centre was of buckets hastily being filled with cold water. The DAC came to see us. (It is the Diocesan Advisory Council which has to vet any proposed change to a church building, from the reupholstering of a *prie-dieu* to the opening of a massage-parlour in the crypt.) I recall that they huddled together rather nervously. Clearly someone had told them about Hackney.

The key paragraph of the brief letter we received from the DAC after their visit is worth quoting:

> 'The building being of immense importance, it is considered essential that the parish personnel (*sic*) come to a proper understanding of the significance of St John-at-Hackney, particularly in relation to the Hackney community before working further on any plans.'

DACs are notorious for communications of this sort. These bodies are dominated by those Philip Larkin described as 'randy for antique', deeply learned men and women, expert in corbels and stoups. Their passion for mission is less conspicuous. It would be interesting to analyse, were there not far better things to do, what they said to us. It would be a fascinating literary exercise to register how skilfully their letter both patronizes and belittles the reader, to note the vacuity of its vocabulary ('immense importance' – importance to whom? – importance for what?) and to savour the audacity of those who – some seeing our church for the first time – claimed to understand it better than those who had loved it and looked after it for decades.

We were not dissuaded from our purpose by this sad letter, which I retain only in the hope that one day it may be anthologized. But the continuing undertow of disquiet about our vision of a new St John's did eventually sap our resolve. The lay people committed to our project came from a world where plans are bold and plans lead to action. They were puzzled by the timidity of the church's culture ('never put off to tomorrow what can be deferred for very much longer'), a disposition which they did not find supported in the New Testament. These good people, some still at St John's, some who have now moved on, are as committed as ever to the cause of Christ. But they know, as I do, that we missed a tide that may never return.

The building had one last sickening body blow for us all before I left the parish. I was called over to the church one morning to find that 'the house was filled with smoke'. This was not, as it had been for Isaiah in the temple, because God had turned up, but because the place was on fire. The cupboard housing all our church's switches, meters, fuse boxes, and other electrical gizmos had gone up in flames. Eyewitnesses said it was as if someone had dropped a lighted match in a box of fireworks. After the fire was extinguished and the smoke had settled as a pall of grey dust on our pews, forensic investigators arrived to investigate what might have caused it. Among them were boffins from the mains suppliers, Électricité de France. Until this catastrophe I had not realized that London's electricity is piped in from Paris. 'Globalization', I think it's called.

The church of St John-at-Hackney has had two serious fires in living memory. The first was in 1955. That inferno left only our walls standing. A feisty lady on the PCC, who witnessed that fire, maintained that such a clearly dysfunctional pile should never have been rebuilt. She had the weird idea that the church is a pilgrim people. This second conflagration, in 2006, was at the start of January. We remained without power, and so without heating and lighting, for almost the rest of the year. Some are 'saved by fire', says the Bible. Certainly the fire brought us closer together. The building is so vast that worshippers can – and often do – sit at inter-galactic distances from each other. Because we had to rope off the smoke-damaged pews at the back, we all had to huddle together near the front. Strangers for years finally become friends. A few of the elderly, fearful of hypothermia on the bitterest Sundays, stopped coming to church. Most just wrapped up warmly and cuddled up closely. People come clutching hot-water bottles, rugs, and Thermoses for post-liturgical beverages. Lumbered too with hymn-books, orders of service, and notice-sheets, they were getting overloaded. I suggested that we could at least dispense with the Thermos flasks if we simply filled our hot-water bottles with tea, coffee, or soup.

The experience of the fire and its aftermath was a mix of the high, the low, and the comic. Highs included swift offers of help. St John's is 'twinned' with Ely cathedral. As soon as they heard of the fire, they offered to meet the cost of hiring heaters. The contraptions we bought in for a few Sundays had all the impact on the air of lighted matches at the North Pole, but they gave a psychological boost and reminded us of our friends in the Fens. My lowest moment came at six o'clock one Sunday morning, in a pitch-black freezing church, as I struggled to attach the butane cylinders to the catalytic heaters. ('Butane', 'catalytic'– note my mastery of the technical terms. My language at the time was more colloquial.)

Comedy came bound in red tape from a sure source of the absurd. The DAC sent someone round to ensure that any measures we took to restore electricity were compliant with Faculty requirements. We were punctilious about such matters at St John-at-Hackney. We held the necessary extraordinary PCC meeting at which we duly resolved 'to petition the Chancellor to grant a faculty permitting the connection of a temporary power supply'. The meeting took place during one of the services, after the blessing and before the last hymn. It lasted fully forty-five seconds.

We shivered in church, but we were not the ones who really suffered. The severest impact of the fire was on the homeless who sleep in the church's porches. Before the fire we were serving them a daily cooked breakfast. That had to stop. The fire was an 'act of God', of course. We preach of 'God's preferential option for the poor' and yet when God acts it is usually the poorest who are most hurt. I find that puzzling.

Too many pages of my Hackney diary were taken up with our intractable building. Well before I left I decided to keep quiet about it. But not before posting one last entry.

I have taken a vow of silence. To be precise, I've decided to stop belly-aching about our building. I notice people yawning when I begin moaning about it yet again. Or they suddenly remember urgent appointments elsewhere. So I shall post this last report and then belt up. The fire was in early January. Three months and a freezing winter later they reconnected the electricity. The power restored proved just enough for an electric toothbrush or a twenty-watt bulb – though not for both at the same time. Ours is about the biggest parish church in London. Providing a current strong enough for such a building, we are told, will mean trenches through the churchyard to carry new high-powered cabling. Oh yes, and then the whole building will have to be rewired. It's clear too that our ancient vicious oil-fired boiler can't be resuscitated. A completely new gas-fired heating-system is needed. More trenches. More labyrinthine bureaucracy. And – oh frabjous day! – lots more faculties.

Like Daniel, I experience night-visions. In these visions I behold our building for what it is. I see a great gaping mouth, opening on a bottomless abyss, a maw which swallows thousands upon thousands upon thousands of pounds, while the poor of Hackney struggle to make ends meet. I behold this monstrous gullet, consuming the time and energy of good Christian people, the saints of St John-at-Hackney whose shoelaces I am not worthy to untie. There is an obvious solution to all these problems. But of that we may not speak. So I'll shut up.

The church of St John-at-Hackney is surrounded by a vast church-yard, one of the many open spaces which make Hackney a surpris-ingly green place to live in. The churchyard has now been restored to something of its former glory. Proposals for its restoration had been made long before I arrived as rector and it was well after I left that the work was finished. The churchyard has long been closed to burials and responsibility for its maintenance and upkeep is the local council's. Long closed to the dead, the churchyard remains a memorial to the fallen, those who gave their lives in two world wars. Each year the civic Remembrance Day service is held in the church and wreaths are placed at the war memorial. The churchyard is Hackney's 'Memorial Gardens'. Alas, for most of my time in Hackney that churchyard was a monument to council neglect. Most days I had reason to wander through the churchyard. It served as a stage-set for many little scenes of inner-city life. Here are some snapshots of those scenes.

The local arsonists who are back at work. Bored with incinerating the skips in the churchyard, they have turned their attention to the cars parked around the church. This morning my path to the church door is blocked by the skeletal remains of a torched Toyota. It looks like the carcase of a buffalo, bones picked dry by Tserengeti hyenas. Someone from the Council has slapped a bright yellow sticker on what was the boot, threatening the owner with prosecution for failing to display a valid road fund licence.

An old sewing machine, a mattress, a kitchen door, an upturned bath, and a broken toilet rest on a pile of rat-ridden decomposing detritus by one of our church porches. (The porch on the other side of the church shelters two or three homeless. Apart from the needles they've finished with, it's much tidier.) I have mixed feelings about these mountains of stinking refuse which accumulate in our churchyard. I suppose I should be shocked that people treat holy ground as a council tip. But then I remember St Paul's words. 'We are,' as he delicately puts it, 'the filth of the world, and the off-scouring of all things unto this day.' In other words we're here to be shat upon.

Anyone want a hearse? A sumptuous white Daimler hearse has been abandoned in our churchyard. It is a magnificent vehicle in immaculate condition. Most cars left in our churchyard are swiftly plundered and torched. This carriage is so grand that it seems our local vandals are shy of touching it. Or perhaps, mindful of the use to which it was put in its working life, they have left it alone for fear of desecration. I love hearses and, now that there are hardly any church funerals, I miss my frequent rides in them. Undertakers are always a fund of succulent gossip. Sitting next to the undertaker at the front of the hearse, on its leisurely journey from church to cemetery, one often learned a thing or two about one's fellow clergy of which one's archdeacon was happily unaware.

Ten minutes after I arrived in Hackney ten years ago the Council approached us about our churchyard. It is our churchyard, but the Council is responsible for maintaining it, an obligation to which they have sat lightly over the years. They asked us whether we would welcome a plan to restore the churchyard and of course we agreed. After a decade of meetings and exchanging bumph, work has at last started. More important than making our churchyard beautiful was the need to make it safe. So, before anything else, something had to be done about the trees. Trees that were dead, dying, or dangerous had to be felled. But the tree surgeons had to take account of more sinister factors. Our churchyard may be consecrated ground, but in its shadows drugs are pushed, sex sold, the elderly mugged, and suicide committed. We can't hold evening events in church in winter, because people find crossing the churchyard after dark too scary. So the bushy trees with low canopies, sheltering the villains and the hanky-panky, had to be pruned. On the morning the work started I went out to welcome the woodsmen. And I walked into a fight – not fisticuffs, but one of those glorious verbal punch-ups which are characteristic of public discourse in the London Borough of Hackney. Trees are very beautiful and only God could have made them, but they do excite the irrational and the love of them is often blind. The protesters I met that morning seemed to think that we were about to destroy the last of the Amazonian rain-forest.

St John-at-Hackney's Memorial Gardens are now once again what once they were. The wilderness now rejoices. The surest sign that the long-departed glory has returned is that children now play in the rose garden behind the church. We may or may not be nearer God's heart in a garden than anywhere else, but gardens still speak to us of where we belong, of the Eden from which we have been so long exiled, and of the paradise we are promised. It's good that Hackney Parish Church is set in a garden.

As for the building, 'the ugliest building in Christendom bar one', it is still there, so far as I know. There is, as I say, an obvious solution to all its problems.

7

Boys and Girls Come Out to Play

The high point in the year for the Hackney Free and Parochial Secondary School is the presentation of 'the Sedgwick medals'. Harry Sedgwick was a 19th century churchwarden who left £500 in his will for fifteen silver medals to be awarded annually to deserving pupils of our parish schools 'as near to the Whitsun holidays as possible and in fine weather'. Nowadays the medals are struck in baser metal and this year the ceremony takes place on a dull day in Lent. The school assembles in church. The communion is celebrated and bread and wine are tendered to the undeserving. By contrast, the medals presented by the Bishop of London at the end of the service have to be earned. They are awarded – so Harry Sedgwick stipulated – to seven boys and (don't ask) eight girls 'for merit'.

Medals for merit must be worn with caution. Saki has the story of the little girl who wins three medals for goodness. The king is so pleased with her that he allows her to visit his park once a week. There she walks, her medals proudly pinned to her dress. One week she sees a wolf prowling in the park. In terror she hides behind a bush, but, alas, the clinking of her medals gives her away, and the wolf hunts her down and devours her. All that's left of her are her three medals for goodness.

I once had a verse from the Bible on the wall of my study. The text – showing off as ever, I had it up in the Hebrew – comes from an Old Testament prophet's vision of the New Jerusalem. 'The streets of the city shall be full of boys and girls playing in the streets thereof' (Zechariah 8.5). I often returned to those words while I was in Hackney. In our inner-cities, as everywhere else these sad days, children are no longer let out to play. If the Christian hope of the kingdom of God is ever fulfilled that will change. Out of doors will

81

no longer be out of bounds. The City of God will be a children's playground. We grown-ups too, if we can reclaim our own childhood as Jesus said we must, will run outside and join them.

The Church of England is confused about children. It engulfs them in clouds of pious fog. It sends them contradictory signals. We claim that all children are equally loved by God, but when it comes to deciding who shall go to one of our schools we show what we really believe, that some children are more equally loved than others. We welcome children into the family of God at their baptism and then refuse them food from our family table. We talk to them about God as if we grown-ups know any better than they do what is beyond words to tell.

In my dealings with our Hackney children, I tried to maintain some sense of direction through these enveloping mists. I attempted to be consistent, coherent, and at least faintly Christian in three contentious areas: the church and its schools, children and Holy Communion, and the disputed borderlands of spirituality and religion. This chapter and the next are about the boys and girls of Hackney. In this chapter I focus on our schools; in the next I recall the children who sometimes came to church.

Most unusually, St John-at-Hackney has two church schools, a primary school and secondary school. Both are 'Voluntary Aided' schools, a status which means that the church continues to have a significant role in the school's governance. As rector, I was *ex officio* a governor of both schools and I drifted in and out of them a lot. Most weeks I conducted – that oddest of offices – the school assembly. Both schools came to church at least once a term. The primary school church services were delightful.

It's our primary school's 'End of Year Celebration'. I stand in the porch to welcome the children, two by two, into church. I feel like Noah at the door of the ark. As in his day, the earth is filled with violence. Like the ark, St John-at-Hackney seems a vessel built by a madman miles from the sea. High above us this very afternoon there are men working on the leaking old tub, pitching it within and without with pitch. I pray that these innocents may be spared what must surely befall the earth. The service begins with a sea-shanty, or what sounds like it, 'Rock my soul in the bosom of Abraham'. The children belt out the wacky words without thinking about them. Not that it matters. There's more to children's worship than reciting the right lines. If what these children are doing is all rather mindless it is no less the real thing. It occurs to me that the child too young to praise with understanding is worshipping no less worthily than the old man too old to praise with cartwheels. I reflect on how the richness of children's worship exposes by contrast the poverty of most of what passes for worship in adult liturgy, worship which we don't let the children join without their going through some eleven-plus rite of passage. Mill-stones await us, we who have created such stumbling-blocks. At the end of the service a small boy asks me, 'Is this your church?' 'No,' I reply. 'It's yours.'

I have many such good memories of our primary school. But the recent history of that school is harrowing. I shared the pain and I need to share the story. What we suffered was the enactment of government educational policy at its most brutal. It is the story of how a sick school was made worse by treatment purportedly intended to make it better. It is the chronicle of how a community was put to death by public execution. It is the record too – for, thank God, this story has a 'third day' – of how a new school arose from the grave of the old one, a school which today is flourishing. Whether our little school had to be crucified so that a better one could be born remains unclear to me. Here is what I wrote when the axe was about to fall:

'Ram's to fold' is the terse headline in the *Hackney Gazette*. The reference is to the Ram's Episcopal Primary School (the name has nothing to do with sheep that safely graze, but preserves the memory of an eighteenth-century Hackney worthy, one Stephen Ram). It seems certain that Ram's, our Voluntary Aided primary school, will technically close on 31 August this year (2000) and reopen, possibly under a different name, on the Sept 1st. In government-speak, the school will make a 'Fresh Start'.

Rams was founded as long ago as 1520. For most of that time, or so it feels, it has been 'on special measures', the government's spooky euphemism for what it deems to be a failing school. In fact we have been wearing this label for nearly five years, certainly some sort of dismal record. Schools that are 'on special measures' are expected to put their house in order within no more than two years or face closure. So we have long known that we have been living on borrowed time.

Alas, the one measure that could save the day for our school is now no longer an option. Anyone with any experience of teaching knows that if a school has problems there is only one solution. You put in a strong head. That head identifies the teachers who are struggling. He or she sees that those willing to learn get all the help they need to do a better job. The obdurate, the idle, and those who have missed their true vocation as market-gardeners have to go. Having appointed a tough head you then – and this is the vital step – get off the school's back.

Previous years for the school had been a *via dolorosa*. No one disputed Ofsted's original decision to place the school 'on special measures'. Undoubtedly there was much amiss. The issue was not whether our primary school deserved the inspectors' damning appraisal. The question mark was over all that the school suffered subsequently. Because there is no doubt that the actions supposedly taken to remedy the school's problems only made matters much worse.

First, after being placed 'on special measures', the school received repeated monitoring visits by the inspectors. It was monitored to death. It is impossible to exaggerate how demoralizing this experience was for the staff. There is something very Old Testament about the scrutiny of Her Majesty's Inspectors. It is all judgement and no grace. I spent eighteen years as a classroom teacher and I know that the surest way to reduce a child to gibbering breakdown is to stand over him or her repeating, 'Not good enough'. Grown-ups are no different and it is no surprise that our teachers found it increasingly difficult to get up from the floor and start again after each successive going-over.

Secondly, the school was publicly pilloried. In 1997 Rams was one of the eighteen schools named by the Secretary of State for Education as being in exceptionally dire straits. We were, as the *Evening Standard* announced, one of 'the dunce schools'. The young David Copperfield was forced to wear the placard, 'This boy bites'. Being publicly humiliated in the way it was did as much good for our little school as that label did for Dickens's hero.

That 'naming and shaming' was unforgivable. As a consequence a number of parents, those with the savvy and clout to work the system, withdrew their children and placed them in better schools. These children tended of course to be the brighter ones. A descending spiral was set in motion. Teachers were expected to achieve the same results with the clever kiddies creamed off. Surprise, surprise, the inspectors were unsatisfied. Consequently more children with get up and go got up and went.

What happened at Rams was not, of course, unique. It was one example of what happens in a competitive educational system designed to train a meritocracy. The result is educational apartheid. Children of parents with oomph all end up in one sort of school. The rest, the most vulnerable and thus the most deserving, end up in another.

All this was going on in Hackney, one of the United Kingdom's most impoverished inner-city boroughs. Hackney children start the educational high hurdles fifty metres behind the starting-line and it is hardly surprising if results do not compare favourably with those achieved in Virginia Water. To be sure, other primary schools in Hackney won the inspectors' wintry smile. Whether Rams was so much worse than those other primary schools is debatable. What is not debatable is that our school was serving a poor place with children presenting multiple problems. No Ofsted or HMI report I saw acknowledged that our staff at least had the bottle to teach in it.

The travails of the Rams Episcopal Primary School highlight and dramatize what continues to take place in all our schools. It is the prioritizing of penultimate quantifiable targets over the ultimate and unquantifiable goal of education – the getting of wisdom. 'Be good, sweet child,' said Charles Kingsley, 'and let who will be clever.' In 1944, through the influence of Archbishop William Temple, it was written into our educational legislation that the spiritual and moral well-being of children should be the goal of their schooling. In our own time we have seen the abandonment of that great vision and its replacement by a raft of measurable targets which, worthy as they are, fall far short of Temple's far richer concept of human flourishing. These days a child at primary school is more likely to be praised for his 'mouse-skills' than commended for his kindness or comforted on the death of a pet rabbit.

I remained sceptical about the 'Fresh Start' process – and in the end all because I had such vivid memories of Norman. I once had to teach eight-year-old Norman mathematics. Norman got all his sums wrong. But he would always write across the top of the next page of his exercise book, in great big capitals, the two words 'FRESH START'. The sentiment was admirable. But it did nothing for his maths.

In the event the 'Fresh Start' route was indeed followed. At midnight on 31 August 2000 Rams Episcopal Primary School ceased to exist. A nanosecond later a new school started on the same site, the St John and St James Church of England Primary School. Builders moved in to refurbish the old premises. At the beginning of the autumn term a largely new staff under a new head teacher was in place. A fresh team of governors took over. (I was the ghost at the table. *Ex officio*, I was governor of the new school as of the old.)

The return of the inspectors was awaited apprehensively. But the first Ofsted report of the new school was very different from those which had traduced the old one. That report did contain the occasional 'could do better', but overall it was a paean of praise. Ofsted reports are generally sober and restrained documents. Those who write them are not given to rhetorical flourishes or purple passages. Her Majesty's Inspectors rarely unbutton. Yet their measured comments, notwithstanding their remarks on 'room for improvement', failed to hide their delight in what they found. You had the sense that they had flung away their clipboards and were dancing round the room.

How are we to account for what happened, for the transformation of a demoralized and under-achieving school into one that today is manifestly happy and flourishing? It won't do to claim that the turn-around simply proves how good the government's 'Fresh Start' strategy is. What they did to the old school had only made bad matters worse. Nothing alters the fact that what the school suffered from the government and its Ofsted enforcers was coarse and callous butchery. It was thanks to the inspirational head teacher who took over, not to the heavy-handedness of the government's educational policy, that things changed.

But perhaps there was another dimension to what took place, a factor far beyond Whitehall's comprehension or control. What our primary school experienced was – to choose a word advisedly – a 'resurrection'. Resurrection is an event in saving history and the promise of the best yet to be. But it is also a present possibility, a principle already at work, 'the deeper magic from before the dawn of time' that out of the graveyard of our day-to-day failures – failing schools among them – new life can be born. I believe in the resurrection of the dead because I saw it happen in Hackney, in a school which, having been cruelly done to death, is now according to the inspectors, their elation cracking the mould of Ofsted prose, 'buzzing with life'.

Because of its travails, I was more closely involved with our primary school than with our secondary school. But I saw enough of Hackney Free and Parochial Secondary School to develop a deep respect for those who teach inner-city teenagers, not all of whom go to school because they want to learn.

'Hackney Free' contrasts with the schools I had taught in, as I noted in my diary.

Our Secondary School has just published its latest 'School Improvement Plan'. Its forty-five pages set out under one hundred and fifty nine headings what has to be done, who has to do it, when it has to be done by, who's to check it's being done, how they're to tell it's being done, and who will say – when it's done – whether it was done properly. This plan has to be coordinated with the school's Post-OFSTED Action plan, its Education Action Zone Plan, its Excellence in Cities Plan, its Behaviour Improvement Plan, its Sports College Plan, and its Leadership Improvement Grant Plan.

Pendulums swing. At the school where I began my teaching career the pendulum was at the other end of its arc. Nothing, but nothing, was planned. I turned up on the first day of term and was told what subjects and classes I was to teach until break. At break I was told who and what to teach until lunch. Over lunch, the Headmaster suggested who might benefit from my wisdom and on what for the rest of the day. To be sure, that school, even in those days, was hardly a model of how schools should be run. (Though an eight-year-old in one of my scripture classes is now the Regius Professor of Moral and Pastoral Theology in the University of Oxford.)

Jesus wasn't much of a planner. The experience of the disciples after his departure was much like mine in that prehistoric prep-school. They were just left to get on with it. As I put my head between my legs to consult the 'Mission Action Plan' pinned to the seat of my trousers, I find that thought encouraging.

First impressions of Hackney Free can be misleading. Razor wire surmounts the perimeter fence. A police officer is permanently seconded to the site. Those more used to how children converse in the suburbs and the shires will wonder why inner-city kids, particularly the girls, apparently cannot talk to each other without screaming. When I conducted school services for all seven hundred children at once I felt as if I was performing the liturgy on the thin crust of an active volcano.

Certainly the school is as tough as any other inner-city comprehensive. Currents of violence springing from dysfunctional home situations sometimes surface in classrooms and corridors. Too many 'students' – especially Afro-Caribbean boys – have small appetite for study. Teachers who can't cope don't stay.

All the more impressive, then, is all the school does for its young people, so many of whom are disadvantaged and potentially disaffected. Perhaps most impressive has been the school's success in channelling constructively energies that could easily have been misdirected. Despite being located on a tiny crowded site with no playing fields, the school has achieved spectacular sporting success. Since 2002 the school has been a 'Sports College'. At the time of writing, Hackney Free are the National Pentathlon Champions.

It is easy to be cynical about the upgrading of schools into 'colleges', just as it is about the renaming of polytechnics as 'universities'. It is also fair to ask – and as someone who was useless at games I do ask – whether athletic success promotes academic achievement. The fact is that, thanks to our school, many Hackney boys and girls now feel they are winners and that must be good.

One year I was asked to give the prizes at Hackney Free's 'Awards Evening'. The invitation sent my wayward mind back to a prize-giving I had to sit through at the school where for many years I was chaplain. I recalled the occasion in my diary.

The prizes were given by an alderman of the City of London. This worthy owned a chain of stores retailing unpleasant furniture. The alderman distributed the prizes and then embarked on an interminable and stunningly boring speech. The afternoon was sultry, the hall stifling, the audience comatose. We were suddenly roused by a flash of lightning and a clap of thunder. Through the floor-to-ceiling windows we saw a drama unfolding. The school nurse was sprinting by. She was a lady of unathletic build and sedentary disposition and the school watched the unfamiliar spectacle with astonishment and fascination. The lightning, we learned later, had struck Wiggins, a third former who, wise lad, had bunked off. The alderman, droning on, noticed nothing. Wiggins quickly recovered. I never have.

My eyes and ears in Hackney Free were Mark's. Mark, the head of Religious Studies, was for many years a professed Benedictine monk. He left his monastery because he found life there too soft. Mark worried as I did about the claim our school made, as every church school does, that it set out 'to implement Gospel values' and 'to create a Christian ethos'. Were these sentiments any more than holy noises, we wondered? I recall an exercise I sometimes set the teenagers I once taught. I asked them to compare the Sermon on the Mount ('Give, and don't expect to be repaid') with the school rules ('Never lend money') and to tell me which of the two codes of conduct they thought they should obey. Pious students told me that we should do what Jesus said. Prudent pupils rightly said that we'd be better advised to obey the headmaster.

The fact is that it is no more possible to run a school than it is to run a country on 'Gospel values', if by those values we mean the distinctive ethic of Jesus – 'take up your cross' – rather than the moral principles that are shared by all people of goodwill, whatever their faith commitment. The mistake that church schools make in their windy words about 'Gospel values' and the like is that they confuse the Christian religion with spirituality. As we saw, William Temple's success in getting something about 'spiritual development' included alongside religious education in the 1944 Education Act was a vital victory. He recognized that the things of the spirit are far too important to be left to religious professionals. He saw that there is a transcendent dimension to all of life and thus to every subject on a school timetable. Everything – the insides of a rabbit, the properties of right-angled triangles, the exports of Peru, the reprehensible misbehaviour of French irregular verbs – is, or should be, a source of wonder. And 'until we have learned to wonder we shall not reign or rest'.

Mark and I agreed that a school which serves a pluralist neighbourhood, which welcomes children of many different religious affiliations, and which is staffed by believers, half-believers, and non-believers, should not pretend to be a confessional community. The common ground for such a school – a church school as much as any other – must be its shared spirituality, not an entirely notional shared Christian commitment. A school affirming a non-confessional spirituality to underpin its common life, a spirituality accessible to those of all faiths or none, is not settling for the second best. Such a spirituality is not necessarily a secular humanist spirituality, nor need it be a 'pick-and-mix' spirituality which trawls the traditions for the edifying and inoffensive but which in fact is a hybrid that none of those traditions would recognize or own. Spirituality – our 'moral awareness of the other and the beyond' – is hard-wired into us. It is how we are constituted. The nurture of the spirit is anything but a dilettante business and it is the most important thing a school can do.

Such was the thinking behind the development which came to fruition shortly after I left Hackney. I wrote about it in my diary.

Don't come back. That's the rule which incumbents must keep when they leave their parish. That being so, I was grateful to Father Rob Wickham, my successor as Rector of Hackney, for letting me come back to Hackney for a momentous occasion. From now on 17 April each year will be remembered as the anniversary of two remarkable events in the history of the western church. For on that day in 1521 Martin Luther appeared before the Diet of Worms. And on that day in 2007 the Bishop of London blessed and dedicated 'The Jerusalem Space' at Hackney Free and Parochial Secondary School.

The Jerusalem Space is what we made of a disused boys' privy off the backstairs of the school. This little room – and it is very small – has now been set apart as a place of quiet, 'the still point of the turn-ing world' of an inner-city comprehensive school. In practice, it will serve as a room for reflection and prayer, as a tiny chapel where bread will sometimes be broken, and at all times and at any time as a place 'for being in'. As a symbol it will point to 'the New Jerusalem', to the city we must seek if our lives are to be more than a futile sequence of wasted days. The space includes a stunning triptych by the great contemporary Christian artist Mark Cazalet, depicting 'Christ the Light of Hackney'. Mark, who delights in mischief, has depicted me in a corner of one of the panels, much as a mediaeval mason, working on a new cathedral, might carve a grotesque gargoyle of some self-important bishop.

You cannot promulgate the sayings of Jesus as school rules. 'If your hand is a nuisance cut it off', 'Sell all you have and give to the poor', 'Don't resist evil'. By such teaching Jesus is not legislating for the corridors and classrooms of an inner-city comprehensive school. There is one way, however, in which a school which presumes to call itself Christian certainly can and should obey the letter of the law of Christ. The tragedy and the scandal is, that by refusing to go this Christian way, most church schools deny the very gospel they exist to affirm.

A day or two before I left Hackney someone called at the rectory with a request I'd heard many times before.

For the last time – pray God, for the last time – a weary Mum, hung about with much shopping and many offspring, calls at my door, pleading that I will sign a form to help get one of her children into one of our schools. For the last time – pray God, for the last time – I hear the grovelling apology, 'I'm afraid that we don't get to church very often.' For the last time – pray God, for the last time – I have to quench my incandescent rage with the iniquitous system that expects parents to pitch up at church to win a place at one of our schools. For all my confusions about Christianity, one thing is clear to me. Christian allegiance cannot confer any rights. All is of grace, nothing is merited. Church schools, like churches themselves, should be for those outside. If there has to be a queue for a limited number of places, this mum should be at the front of it. So I tell her, just as I've told countless other mums, that at our church we don't take a register, that I'll certainly sign her form, and that anyway she needn't worry because, as a governor, I've made very sure that the admissions criteria for our schools do not exclude children like hers. Yes, we have a 'church attendance' criterion, but all it stipulates is that the family must come to church 'regularly'. I point out that she will fully comply with this criterion if she comes to church with her kiddies at Christmas every other leap year.

Jesus of Nazareth preached good news to the poor. The Church of England preaches a different gospel to parents wanting a place for their child at a church school. The church's gospel to such parents is bad news to the poor. Its gospel is very bad news indeed to a single mum on a sink estate, struggling to cope on income support, a mum for whom the task, on top of everything else, of getting herself and the kids to church on Sunday is impossible. By contrast the Church of England's gospel is good news to the well off. It is good news to middle-class parents with the savvy to play the system, to those who can get to church and get themselves noticed when they get there.

Nowhere is the Church of England more compromised, nowhere is its practice at a greater distance from the ethic of the kingdom of God, than in the 'preferential option for the rich' that it exercises in deciding who shall have places in its schools. The sure route to the front of the queue for a place for your child at a sought-after church school is to be there in church Sunday by Sunday. Better still, sing in the choir, arrange the flowers, launder the linen – the opportunities to put yourself about and to catch the vicar's eye are endless. Any qualms about saying you believe in God can be swiftly suppressed. No sacrifice is too great to secure that vital 'church letter'. If necessary, get yourself confirmed. Kneeling before the bishop, you can always keep your fingers crossed behind your back.

The heresy which shapes the Church of England's policy on admissions to its schools is to suppose that Christian affiliation secures *entitlements*, that it is to your advantage to profess to be a Christian. To assist governors of church schools in deciding who shall have places and who shall not, the National Society has come up with what they commend as a simple series of criteria, 'a three-tier stratification for faith-based places'. To assess the level of commitment parents might have to their local church, governors are encouraged to ask whether the parents are 'known to the church', 'attached to the church', or 'at the heart of the church'. The criteria may be simple but they are certainly not Christian. Were we to allow the ethic of Jesus to modify the National Society's 'stratification', we would have to add a fourth tier – 'unknown to the church'. So, in addition to the three tiers of 'insiders', we would have a tier of 'outsiders' too. You do not have to read very far in the gospels to notice which cohort of humanity Jesus was most at home with and which most fully satisfied the admissions criteria of his kingdom.

If we must use the language of 'rights', surely church schools, like the church itself, should exist precisely for those who have no rights, who do not 'deserve' to belong to them. Church schools should be like heaven. You don't get in by going to church. I never quite persuaded my fellow-governors to announce in the school's prospectus that, in allocating places, priority would be given to 'the children of publicans and sinners'. But perhaps that would not have been a good idea. We had so many of those in Hackney that our schools would still have been over-subscribed.

8

Let my Children in

I shall not forget my first Midnight Mass in Hackney. Seven year old Judy was entrusted with baby Jesus and, to the singing of 'Away in the Manger', she led the procession to the crib. Her contribution to the liturgy, not prescribed by the rubric, was to drop him. 'Never mind, Judy,' I whispered. 'We'll pick him up.' 'We can't, 'she announced. 'His head's come off. It's gone under the piano.' I could hear people singing – it seemed very far away – about someone who 'lay down his sweet head' and I briefly wondered, as I scrabbled under the piano, whether from the pulpit I could turn this catastrophe to advantage. But it was a line of thought I did not pursue. Much more urgent was the question of whether there was any Sellotape in the vestry.

Children do not behave in church, any more than anywhere else, in the way grown-ups wish. Their capacity to disrupt worship is boundless. But worship isn't just what children disturb. It is also what they do.

Our primary school crocodiles to church for its Harvest Festival. For once our vast spaces are filled with an abundance of life. Their voices soar to our dilapidated vaulting,

> 'There are hundreds of children, thousands and millions,
> But God knows everyone and God knows me.'

Artless prayers, led by year six, are as true as a bell. Harvest gifts are brought in procession to the altar. A small boy hands over his packed lunch. By the end of the service I am close to tears. We, so swift to judge these little ones, are not worthy to stoop down and loosen the laces of their Reebok trainers.

Children have their own distinct ways of worship. Both their capacity to upset the liturgical applecart and the authenticity of their own worship are illustrated by a story in the gospels that we often miss. This is what Matthew says happened when for the last time Jesus entered the Temple in Jerusalem:

> The blind and the lame came to him at the temple, and he healed them. But when the chief priests and the teachers of the law saw the wonderful things he did and the children shouting in the temple area, 'Hosanna to the Son of David', they were indignant. 'Do you hear what these children are saying?' they asked him. 'Yes,' replied Jesus, 'have you never read, "From the lips of children and infants you have ordained praise"?' (Matthew 21.14–16)

This incident fascinates me. Most religions – and most conspicuously Christianity – marginalize children. Belief systems and patterns of worship have always been adult constructs. Any part conceded to children in the community's religious life has always been strictly regulated by adults. Yet Jesus here welcomes the spontaneous outburst of the children, so threatening to the Dean and Chapter of the Temple, and affirms it as acceptable worship. It is of a piece with his insistence that children should be at the centre of the community he gathered round him and that they are the kind of people we must be if we are thinking of becoming his followers.

Jesus' estimate of children – what he said about them and how he treated them – has shaped my whole ministry. Forty years ago I wrote a thesis about Jesus and children entitled *The New Testament Theology of Childhood*. (It was published, unhelpfully for anyone who lived anywhere else, in Hobart, Tasmania.) In that study I tried to show that Jesus' estimate of children is not based on the 'childlike' qualities we like to attribute to them – their openness, trustfulness, spontaneity, insight, and the rest – but on their helplessness. Like the poor and downtrodden to whom Jesus reached out at every step of his way, children – helpless to help themselves – live by grace, human and divine. The disciples vie with each other for highest status in Christ's coming kingdom. That status, Jesus teaches, belongs to those who have no status at all.

Jesus said that God's kingdom belongs to children. They do not have to be 'won for Christ'. They are already his. The notion of 'children's evangelism' is a nonsense. Jesus placed a child among his disciples as a pattern of what they should become. He taught that, in receiving a child, we receive him and the one who sent him.

In our church at Hackney we tried to obey those principles by setting children at the heart of our life and worship. In attempting to do so we found that we were going against the tide. These days the Church of England wants to have everything and everyone under control including, it seems, its children.

One of the ways in which an institutional religion tries to keep children in their place is by excluding them, at least until puberty, from full participation in its rites and rituals. The Church of England does this by imposing on children strict terms and conditions with which they must comply before they are allowed to receive communion at celebrations of the Eucharist. Once there were 'guidelines' in this matter. These now have been upgraded to 'regulations'. I fulminated about them in the *Church Times*.

Something strange will happen in a church near you this Sunday. A priest will read aloud a story from a big book about a teacher who put a child in the middle of his disciples. He will proclaim how this teacher embraced the child, how the teacher said that to welcome such a child was to welcome him – indeed, that to welcome a child was to welcome God. The people will hear that those who do not welcome children deserve to be drowned. The reading of this story will be surrounded by pomp and circumstance. There will be a procession before it is read and the priest will bathe the book in incense. At the end of the reading the book will be held high. The priest will tell the people that what they have heard is good news from God and they will respond with a shout of praise. You will get the impression that this story is meant to be taken seriously.

Which makes what will shortly follow so very peculiar. The priest will invite people to gather round a table to share in a simple meal of bread and wine in remembrance of this man who welcomed children. Timothy, just six years old, will be among those who come to the table. Timothy will hold up his cupped hands, looking forward to receiving a piece of bread like everybody else. But he will be disappointed. The priest will ignore Timothy's request for bread. To be sure, the priest will have a blessing for him, but Timothy will know that this is second best. Perhaps later the priest will explain to Timothy why he was missed out. Perhaps he will tell Timothy that it's all because his name isn't on a little list kept in the vestry, 'the register of children admitted to communion, to be available to be inspected by the Archdeacon at a parochial visitation'. Possibly the priest will explain to Timothy that he keeps this little list because 'regulations', issued by the Arch-bishops' Council, tell him he must. Timothy won't be quite old enough to ask why 'the regulations' are not processed round the church and sensed instead of the big book if, as it seems, they're more important.

On the issue of the admission of children to Holy Communion the Church of England has lost the plot even more spectacularly than it has on the issue of admission of children to its schools. There is a place for the child at the table and bread for him or her to eat – but only if their name is on a list that the archdeacon can look at. If Jesus were not risen from the dead he would be turning in his grave.

Sooner or later Anglican equivocation about the status of chil-dren in the church will drive me into the arms of Orthodoxy. (Already my beard is long enough.) I recall my introduction to the Orthodox liturgy in a church somewhere in the suburbs of Leningrad (as it then was) long before the collapse of communism. The building with room for a thousand was packed with twice that number. The worship was intense, the singing rising like a great tide bearing the griefs and longings of all the Russias. When the time came for communion to be administered such was the surge forward that I feared that the many children present would be trampled underfoot. I need not have worried. They were allowed to squeeze through to the front; toddlers were passed from one willing pair of hands to another across the heads of the people; space was made for the mother with an infant in her arms. And the very youngest received the bread and wine.

One of the requirements in the new regulations on children's admission to communion is that children thus to be admitted should 'be old enough to attend and understand a preparation course'. Those who aspire to Holy Orders have to go on 'selection conferences'. If I were a selector I would invite candidates to offer a theological commentary on that requirement. What they had to say would be quite enough to show whether they should be recommended for ordination or be put on the next train home.

It is tempting to cite these appalling 'regulations' in full. The language of them ('without prejudice to the validity of any permissions already granted thereunder') perfectly illustrates the managerial mind-set that now controls the Church of England. Presumably in some airless office in Church House, Westminster, distracted neither by children nor by what Jesus said about them, there is a would-be lawyer paid to compose such pomposities. When I first read these rules I did not know whether to laugh or to weep or to wander across Hackney marshes with straw in my hair.

No one can pursue a career as a Church of England cleric without sooner or later having conscientious misgivings about some aspect or other of what one is required to do. Nine times out of ten one suppresses one's conscience and does as one is told. But on the tenth occasion, some residual sense of what Christianity actually says forbids further compromise. Regulations which deny children the bread of life unless their names are on some list plainly have to be broken.

Needless to say at St John-at-Hackney we made it clear that children of any age would be welcome at the Lord's Table and that the bread was theirs too. There were no conditions, none whatsoever. I did not ask if the toddler, holding up his hands to me so eagerly, had been baptized. The Galilean children whom Jesus set in his nascent church, whom he commended to his followers as exemplars of discipleship, and with whom he identified himself, were not first required to go through some rite of passage or to sit a test in Religious Knowledge. Their names were not on any list. In Hackney, we were determined to be equally inclusive and welcoming at our communion services. We did not worry overmuch whether the children receiving the sacrament were doing so with sufficient recollection and reverence. I am sure that I have never been that pious myself. It simply seemed to us that those who receive the bread with such manifest delight may be presumed to receive it worthily.

The Christian Eucharist is a meal. It is, we say, the Lord's Supper. It *originated* as a meal. Its context was the celebration of the Passover meal and it was continuous with the regular meals Jesus shared with the crowds that flocked after him. It *continues* as a meal, however vestigial are the traces of food and drink in the token morsel of bread and the sip of wine. The Eucharist will be *consummated* as a meal, the feast in heaven, the messianic banquet when all God's children will eat at his table and the long-promised party at last gets going. The question – and only to ask it is to know the answer – is whether children are excluded from this meal.

The Eucharist originated as a meal. We think of the feeding of the five thousand. John's account has some details which are often overlooked (John 6.1–14). Only John mentions the boy, whom the disciple Andrew has noticed, with his loaves and fish. The word translated 'boy' occurs just this once in the New Testament. In the Greek it is a 'double diminutive'. Here we have not 'a little boy', but rather 'a very little boy'. (Not that we can be certain that the child was male. My seriously unreconstructed dictionary tells me that the word can refer to 'even a female'.) We need a rubber stamp with Andrew's words on it in huge capitals: THERE IS A CHILD HERE! (We might add, 'In case you hadn't noticed.') This admonition then needs to be imprinted across this page of the Bible, as across many another where children have been written out of the story.

The child in this story invites us to reconsider the Eucharist from his or her perspective. John has no account of 'the institution of the Eucharist'. Instead he portrays the feeding of the five thousand as a dramatic sign of Jesus as the bread of life. For John, past and future meet in the sharing of this meal. At this repast, manna in the wilderness is recalled and the feast in heaven anticipated. And it all starts with the child. With the gift of a child the hungry are fed. This wonder takes place, John tells us, at Passover. We recall the role of the child at Passover. Without the questions the child asks, the feast cannot even begin. So with the miracle of the loaves and fish. Nothing happens until the child's presence is acknowledged and the child's gift received. What one child offers becomes bread for all. The interesting question arises as to whether this little Galilean child himself, herself, gets a bit of the bread so marvellously multiplied. I like to think so. Fortunately regulations about 'The Admission of Baptised Persons to Holy Communion', as set out in paragraph 1(c) of Canon B15A of the Canons of the Church of England, had not yet come into force.

I recognize that on this topic I could bore for England, as I was aware when I tried to persuade a clerical colleague, who clearly disapproved of our undisciplined and uncanonical approach to the Holy Mysteries, that there is some theological sense to what we were doing. I invited him to consider the case of the expectant mother who comes to the communion rail. She is, quite literally, carrying a child. Her food is food too for her unborn child. The child to be born, no less a child because yet unborn, is already receiving the body and blood of Christ. I reminded my friend that our first church is our mother's womb. It is there that grace, and, in the sacrament, the means of grace, sustains us. I went on to suggest – although by now my colleague was edging away – that it is much the same with the mum still breast-feeding her baby. The sacrament given to her is received by her baby too. How very odd – I put it to my friend, who now wished he'd never raised the matter – how very odd that we excommunicate children for no other reason than that have been born or weaned.

THE INNER-CITY OF GOD

The word must have got round that this was a subject I was only too ready to talk about, and that, once switched on, I could be relied on to carry on until told to stop. I reflected in my diary on one platform I was called on to mount.

> I was delighted to be asked to be the 'weaver' at this year's Diocesan Children's Advisers' Conference. (A new role for me – I am not known for my knitting.) The last time I spoke at this event was nearly thirty years ago. On that occasion we shared the facilities at Swanwick with a conference, conducted entirely in Esperanto, on eastern European steam trains. I recall the delegates, sad little men with the grey pinched features of those who have stood too long with their grubby notebooks and stubby pencils at the end of Platform 4 of Gdansk Central. We were on fire in those days with a programme, rigorously researched and road-tested, which we were sure would soon have our churches chock-a-block with children. The pro-gramme – *Alive in God's World* we called it – reflected the views of the educational psychologist Ronald Goldmann. Goldmann maintained that children cannot think conceptually, that the Bible is not a chil-dren's book, and that you should never, never, talk to children about sheep unless they've grown up on a farm. Alas, *Alive in God's World* is now one with Nineveh and Tyre.
>
> I enjoyed this year's conference hugely. Children, the great theolo-gian Jürgen Moltmann says, are 'signs of hope' for the church. So too are diocesan children's advisers and I told them as much. Though I did learn something that made me want to stumble back to my room, draw the curtains, and curl up on my bed in a foetal position with my thumb in my mouth and a cold compress on my forehead. Apparently the suits want to impose on us a 'common curriculum', a schedule of what every well-instructed young Anglican should know by the age of eleven. I gather that there are four set-texts to be got by heart: the Lord's Prayer, the Summary of the Law, the Beatitudes – and one more which I forget. That last one will no doubt be a list, in alphabetical order, of the members of the Archbishops' Council.

In its attempts to regulate children's worship more strictly, the Church of England has been curbing what needs to be cultivated –

the spirit of the child. We now know that we are born spiritual. Hard empirical evidence has demonstrated this. To repeat what was said in the last chapter, our spirituality may well be expressed in the language of a religious tradition but it does not have to be. We reach for 'the other and the beyond', whether or not we articulate that spirituality in the language of a faith. Research has shown what the poets have always known, that our spirituality is particularly acute and sensitive in childhood. That spirituality must be nourished. Allowed to atrophy it will wither and die.

As we saw, these are matters debated far beyond church circles. Educationalists now address the spiritual. Schools are required by law to promote the 'spiritual development' of their pupils, a requirement not sufficiently satisfied by RE lessons and school assemblies. Education in all its aspects must have a spiritual dimension to it or it ceases to be true learning. The church is only slowly catching up with this debate.

That said, the Diocesan of London in my time was blessed with a Children's Adviser who saw the need for the church to provide more for its children than entertaining materials for its Sunday Schools. Mary Hawes, now the Church of England's National Children's Adviser, recognized that faith can flourish only if the deep tap-roots of the spirit are nourished. Mary invited me to take part in a diocesan study-day on children's spirituality.

Wordsworth said that children are born 'trailing clouds of glory'. Was he on to something? Or, so daft is the idea, was he on something, out of his head like his friend Coleridge addled with pot and hallucinating about Xanadu? The Wordsworthian belief that children come from God and that they have not yet quite forgotten their first home is now generally derided as sentimental slush. But there are still some late-flowering romantics around who wonder whether something behind the idea is true. 'Trailing Clouds of Glory' was the title of a recent diocesan conference on children's spirituality for which a surprising number of us misty-eyed mastodons signed up. I was asked to speak to the title 'Just tell them stories.' So I did just that. I read *The Whale's Song* and *Old Turtle, Angus Rides the Goods Train* and *Giraffes can't Dance*. Yes, we talked about what these wonderful tales might mean. But of course there is really only one response to the question, 'What's this story saying?' and that is to tell it again. That's why the 'explanations' of the parables in the gospels are clearly secondary glosses, bolted on later by a church, then as now, mistrustful of the imagination.

'Just tell them stories' – the advice is Philip Pullman's, one of the few didactic comments which occasionally punctuate his tremendous trilogy *His Dark Materials*. A year or two ago, I enthused about Pullman in a talk I gave at the International Conference on Children's Spirituality.

> I started a fight – or at least a warm discussion – with a paper about the 'liberation spirituality' of *His Dark Materials*. I said – and it was this that caused the argument – that those who see Pullman's trilogy as an attack on the Christian church simply have not read it attentively. Pullman presents the familiar stereotype of a church obsessed by the sins of the flesh and opposed to unfettered enquiry. With fulminations about gay bishops and baying for heresy trials loud in our ears, Pullman's picture rings true. But it is not the whole truth. For all its shameful history, the church has here and there done a little good and has included, along with the rest of us, one or two quite nice people. Pullman, I argued, counts on a little more sophistication in his readers. His aim is not to pillory the church, though he himself has no time for it. We need to ask what the church as Pullman portrays it stands for, what is the real enemy in all the worlds – whether or not they have churches. That enemy is whoever or whatever constrains the free spirit and stops children – and those no longer children – from growing in love. Outside the garden shed where he writes Pullman has had far more to say about the damage done to children by a prescriptive educational system than about the harm done to them by institutional Christianity. So – since you asked – I'd be perfectly happy to give *His Dark Materials* as a confirmation present.

Conferences, like the parallel universes of *His Dark Materials*, are themselves worlds of their own and re-entry from them into what we loosely call 'reality' can be traumatic. That year's conference, held in Lincoln, was no exception.

> The smart thing to do when travelling from Lincoln to London is to take a taxi to Newark to pick up a mainline train. I shared a taxi with Jerome Berryman, only begetter of 'Godly Play'. Our driver was an enormous skinhead with no neck, terrifying tattoos, and cutlery through his earlobes. A luminous green plastic skull nodded and grinned at us from the dash-board. The speakers behind our heads pumped out something heavy and horrible. (Could this be 'garage', I wondered.) It was a baking hot afternoon. Ten minutes into the journey we ground to a halt. There was an accident ahead. For an hour we hardly moved. 'Do you mind if I smoke?' our chauffeur asked. We did and we said so. Jerome was suffering. We both were. Eventually we took a not-so-short cut through a housing estate. ('Only ten percent are blacks but they spoil it for the rest,' our driver told us.) It was one of those experiences that make you cry out for the Second Coming.

I have attended most of these annual conferences on children's spirituality since they started. Here is what I said in my diary about the first of them.

> I attended – I have the T-shirt to prove it – this summer's 'First International Conference on Children's Spirituality' at University College Chichester (Bishop Otter College, as was). The event brought together a rich and potentially fissiparous mix of high-octane academics, children's advisors, rabbis, advocates of 'Godly Play', and assorted mavericks, stowaways, new-age fruitcakes, and odd-balls like myself. The fact that it didn't all unravel, that it was both so very stimulating and such huge fun, was all down to the good humour and infinite sagacity of the organisers – let them be named and acclaimed! – Clive Erricker, Jane Erricker and Cathy Ota.

One of the most fascinating presentations at that first conference was on 'the contribution of playground songs to children's moral and spiritual growth'. (Such songs, we learn, make the most of the happy circumstance that 'vicars' rhymes with 'knickers'.) The counter-culture of the playground voiced in these marvellous incantations is, it seems, as vibrant as ever. Thank God for that. It is also more important than ever. The playground has become almost the last place in the school where there is any sustained resistance to the fundamentalist ideology of current educational policy, to the dogma that schools are essentially for the force-feeding of commercially useful information. In the playground, if nowhere else, childhood is still affirmed, 'the continuous now' of the child's life celebrated, and the truth made manifest that the measure of my humanity is not my SATS results but who I am.

> 'Row, row, row the boat,
> Gently down the stream.
> Tip your teacher overboard.
> Listen to her scream.'

No wonder some educational mandarins, unnerved by such music, propose cutting back on play-time to allow 'the numeracy hour' to be extended.

The mention of 'Godly Play' allows me to pay tribute to Jerome Berryman and to the approach to the Christian nurture of children which he devised and which he has been teaching for decades.

> The story-teller gathers the children in a small circle round him. He takes his shoes off and sits in the circle with them. He places a box – a beautiful gold-painted box – at the centre of the circle. Very slowly and deliberately – for who knows what secrets this box holds? – he opens it. He takes out a green cloth, carefully unfolds it and lays it out at the centre of the circle. 'I wonder what could be so green?' he asks. 'Grass', a child suggests. The story-teller agrees. 'Yes, it could be grass, but then again it could be a lily-pad or perhaps a leaf from a giant tree.' The story-teller now places a patch of blue cloth on the green. Again his movements are measured. 'I wonder' – the two words are the ground-bass of this story – 'I wonder. Is it a drop on the leaf? Is it a piece of fallen sky? Is it a pool?' Now two or three darker patches are

added. These, the story-teller suggests, are scary. Now some brown strips of cloth are laid down to form a square. 'What can this be, I wonder?' All becomes clear when, with the same deliberation, a little wooden sheep is placed on the cloth. Then more sheep. Then the wooden figure of a shepherd. So the story takes its quiet course. Until at last we hear about the good shepherd who says, 'I count each one of my sheep as they go into the fold and if any are missing I go out and look for them.' The story-teller reflects, 'I wonder if you are searching for the good grass? I wonder if you have ever been lost? I wonder if you have ever been found?'

At St John-at-Hackney we didn't use 'Godly Play', if only because it is a strictly choreographed programme which requires children to be there at the start of each session. In Hackney very few, children or adults, are there for the start of anything – certainly not for church. But I hope that we learned enough from Jerome for his wisdom to inform what we did with our children.

The order of service says that it is time for the sermon. So I sit down on a hassock in the aisle. I invite the children to join me. We all sit higgledy-piggledy in a comfy circle. I tell the children that I am going to tell them a story and that the grown-ups can listen too, but only if they're good. I tell them about Jim who was four. Jim was on his way to the shops with his Mum and Dad. Across the road Jim sees a big crowd of people. He's curious. 'What's going on?' he wonders. He drags Mum and Dad across the road to find out. They're all huge grown-ups in the crowd. So what does Jim do? He does what we all did when we were small and we couldn't see. He wriggles and elbows and shoves and pushes and pushes and shoves and elbows and wriggles until he gets to the front. Then he stops. There in front of him is a man with a kind face. Jim says to the man, 'Hello. My name's . . .' But before he can say any more rough hands grab him and cruel voices start shouting. 'Clear Off!' they shout. 'He's not interested in kids!' The kind man suddenly looks cross. 'Stop!' he says sternly. 'Let the children come to me. I want to be friends with them as well.'

'Godly Play' is a term that sometimes puzzles people. It shouldn't do, for a child at play is very close to God. Watch children playing – register the exuberance, the creativity, the joy of what is happening – and you see what God was doing when the world was made. Jerome Berryman asks somewhere, 'Is God a play-group?'

Children will play in the streets of the New Jerusalem. Meanwhile there's church on Sunday, much as last week, much as next week. What is so predictable can easily go stale. That is why we need our children there and why they must be allowed to play – *to play* – their part in what goes on. What can seem disruptive, because it departs from the grey letter of a printed rite, can be the divine spark that at last brings worship to life. It is something we discovered one Easter.

As Rector of Hackney I have a handsome vestry befitting my high office. The room is furnished to impress on my congregation how important I am. There is an immense desk and behind it a chair as imposing as any bishop's stall. At present this chair is occupied by an enormous Winnie-the-Pooh. This noble beast, altogether too august an animal to be called a teddy-bear, is to be raffled in aid of our 'fabric fund'. For the family service on Easter Day Winnie-the-Pooh is translated from the vestry to the front pew. Someone asks whether he is the new curate. I explain that curates are now virtually extinct. People are shy about sitting near Pooh apart from four-year-old Abigail who, sensing his loneliness, snuggles up beside him. Later, chastened by the charity of this child, many exchange the Peace with Pooh.

As I do so myself, I recall the last of the Pooh stories. At the end Christopher Robin and Winnie-the-Pooh set off together, we know not whither. Lest our hearts should break, A. A. Milne adds a postscript. 'Wherever they go,' he tells us, 'and whatever happens to them on the way, in that enchanted place at the top of the forest a boy and his bear will always be playing.' Of the truth of that claim – agnostic as I am about so much else – I have no doubt at all.

9

God of Surprises

The Alsatian leaps up at my daughter. This hound of the Baskervilles guards a family of asylum seekers living in a house at the bottom of our rectory drive. I decide that the principle of solidarity with the oppressed does not extend to allowing my family to be savaged by wild dogs. I phone the police. A little later a woman police officer is beating on their door with her helmet. No one is at home apart from the beast itself, which hurls itself at the inside of the door in a frenzy. There is a glimpse through the letter box of a slavering jaws and bared teeth. Eventually various members of the household appear. Many speak at once in a language I do not understand. To my shame, I raise my voice. Curious passers-by pause to watch the drama, including one of my churchwardens who seems to think that I am about to be arrested. The conclave concludes with the family agreeing to get rid of the dog. I am, as always, impressed by the extraordinary courtesy of the police. *Blessed are the peacemakers, for they shall be called the children of God.*

The priest who 'passed by on the other side', ignoring the injured figure across the road, probably did so because he had things to do. He had other plans – including, no doubt, a 'Mission Action Plan'. Such plans are fine so long as they can be torn up when necessary. Life in the inner-city is so rich in surprises that parish priests who insist on sticking to their plans are likely to miss many opportunities – and most of the fun – of urban ministry. Much of my Hackney diary is a record of attempts to make some sense of the unexpected.

The prevailing wisdom in the Church of England is that such a strategy is mistaken. The church in every age has its fashionable orthodoxies and heresies which have little to do with what you do or do not believe about the Trinity or the divinity of Christ. One prevailing orthodoxy, from which dissent is not to be countenanced, is that every parson and every parish should have a plan and keep to it. Targets must be set. Timetables must be drawn up. Such and such must be done by so and so by such and such a date. The difficulty with this orthodoxy is that it ignores Tolstoy, the testimony of the prophets, and – that trying man – Jesus of Nazareth.

War and Peace is probably too long a novel for most of today's clergy, 'the few of whom the many expect too much'. But a case could be made for making an annual re-reading of it mandatory so that we might be constantly reminded of Kutuzov, the Russian Commander-in-Chief ('his grey head bent and his heavy body slumped') who understood so well how little command we ever have over what is going to happen. Kutuzov knew that the outcome of the battle is determined not by the dispositions of the commander-in-chief, nor the place where the troops are stationed, nor the number of canon or the multitude of the slain, but by that intangible force called the spirit of the army.

It was Napoleon, the commander who had it all planned, who was defeated.

The notion that we can anticipate what is going to happen is also – to use an old-fashioned evangelical word – unscriptural. The prophets of the Bible had to combat the illusion that you know what God is up to. On the contrary, they say, God is always going to do 'a new thing', precisely what you could never have foreseen:

'From now on I will tell you of new things, of hidden things unknown to you.
'They are created now, and not long ago. You have not heard of them before today. So you cannot say, "Yes, I knew of them."' (Isaiah 48. 6–7.)

Jesus illustrated how he planned his mission with a simple parable. 'The kingdom of God,' he said, 'is as if someone would scatter seed on the ground' (Mark 4.26). By modern standards that is an absurdly inefficient method of farming. The Parable of the Sower highlights just how unproductive it is. The sower throws a handful of seed into the wind in the forlorn hope that some will land on fruitful soil and germinate. Three-quarters of the seed is wasted. As a model for mission it is ludicrous, as laughable as the efforts of the Victorian evangelists who, in the early days of the railways, disseminated the gospel by scattering tracts from the windows of speeding trains.

Yet the text stands and it is an indictment of us. Across the meticulously managed landscape of our modern church there wanders this lonely farmhand, tossing seed in the air. Despite us, the seed grows. He doesn't know how. We don't know how. We love to think we do. Hence the flood of publications about how to grow the church; hence all our Mission Action Plans and the like – but really we haven't a clue. It is all a great mystery. To admit that is not a cop-out. It is to heed the word of the Lord who teaches us that his kingdom and the manner of its growth are precisely that – a *mystery* (Mark 4.10).

Someone said, 'Life is what happens to you when you're making other plans'. That was my experience in Hackney. Often what happened was the unexpected caller.

Shakespeare is buried in our churchyard. That is to say the true author of his plays, Edward de Vere, seventeenth Earl of Oxford, is buried in our churchyard. There is no doubt about the matter according to the self-assured American standing on my doorstep. Not that he is long on my doorstep. 'Can I use your john?' he says and he's off down the corridor. Soon he's settled comfortably in our sitting room deep in *Simpson's Monuments of Hackney Church,* one of the racier titles from my shelves. Apparently we have all been duped. William Shakespeare could not possibly have written the works ascribed to him. 'Shakespeare couldn't even write his name,' my visitor assures me. He is deeply wounded and very angry that de Vere has never got the credit due to him and he is determined that justice shall at last be done. On Sunday he joins us in church. While we sing and pray and do the things people do to pass the time during divine service, he strides round the building inspecting the memorials. Not that any facts forthcoming would be likely to sway a mind so comprehensively made up.

At other times the call which disrupted what I had planned to do came from our day centre for Hackney's homeless.

I am alerted to an emergency in the soup-kitchen. (A free bowl of chunky soup is one of the provisions of our week-day drop-in centre which occupies our south transept.) Someone has claimed to smell gas. The fact is that we have not been connected for gas since the days of Bishop Winnington-Ingram. However facts proved less persuasive than the pong and everyone insisted on summoning the gas-man. He duly turned up with his canary in a cage and crawled all over the church. Poor man, it was like being asked to locate a gas-leak in Gormenghast. And all in vain – not a trace of it. I was about to suggest that we evacuate the premises and phone the fire-brigade. But at that point Alec our sacristan appeared. Alec has the gift of discernment (and countless other gifts, but that's a story for another day). He took one breath and muttered one word – 'Garlic'. Problem solved. Panic over. Someone in the kitchen had garnished the soup too liberally. Unless the garlic was being used for some other purpose. Demons flee, they say, at the first whiff of it. Perhaps some 'deliverance' ritual was in progress. But who or what would they want to exorcise? Why is everybody looking at me?

One morning I was preparing a sermon – in my experience, always an invitation to be interrupted – when I gradually became aware of a disturbance outside.

Glancing through my study window, I notice that the garden is full of firemen. Corporal Jones takes command and I run from room to room urging everyone not to panic. In fact it is not the Rectory which is burning but an abomination just over our garden wall in the churchyard. This disgusting eyesore was a public convenience for the ten minutes which elapsed before the vandals moved in. It has long cried to heaven for the good offices of a dedicated arsonist. When the council built it they drove a Hackney carriage through every rule in the book about what you may and may not do in a disused burial ground. ('Faculty? What's a faculty?') From the day of my induction I have been fighting to get it demolished. (Once upon a time I had a loftier vision of how my days as a priest would be spent, but let that pass.) To my fury the fire-brigade quickly quenches the flames. What can I now say to them which will be 'at once mutually comprehensible, charitable, and true'? Miss Prothero comes to my rescue; old Miss Prothero whose house caught fire one Christmas day and who always said the right thing; dear Miss Prothero who, Dylan Thomas tells us, peered at the handsome firemen standing in the charred ruins of her drawing-room and said, 'Would you like anything to read?'

Our rectory garden was a great joy to us. There was about an acre of it, an oasis in an urban wilderness. The garden used to be much bigger, but that was long ago when the Rector of Hackney had his own butler as well as an army of curates. I hope that we shared our garden enough with others to justify the time we spent in it. When we arrived it was the East End's last area of primary rainforest. My predecessor had done little to it, for the good reason that he was out and about in the parish so much. We tamed the jungle and, though it was never very tidy, it was a delight to us and to those we welcomed into it. You are not necessarily nearer God's heart in a garden, but nevertheless gardens speak of the garden we miss and the garden we are made for. We delighted in our garden, though even there we had not counted on 'the God of surprises'.

Shortly after my induction as Rector of Hackney a length of our garden wall collapsed. ('A sign, brother Pridmore, a sign.') Our garden wall was very old, listed as well as listing. Getting it repaired is proving the most enormous palaver, involving the diocese, English Heritage, and the bureaucracy, none more esoteric, of Hackney

Borough Council. A fierce letter from English Heritage puts paid to any notion that mending our wall is a morning's work for a jobbing bricky and his mate. ('The mortar should be pointed flush and then tamped with a stiff bristle brush to compress the mortar face only so as to reveal the arrises of the bricks.')

I am distressed that our lovely wall is broken. I wonder why I'm so sad about it. I think it can only be because a walled garden is an image of all we have lost and still long for. Our craving is to be again within those unbreached walls, beneath those trees, beside those waters. This nostalgia for paradise is fed by countless springs, by the image of Guillaume de Lorris in the *Romance of the Rose* approaching the enclosed garden, aching to possess its mysteries; by the deep magic of Francis Hodgson Burnett's *The Secret Garden*, (the book, not the schmaltzy film); by the thrilling peroration of Lewis's sermon, *The Weight of Glory* ('Some day, God willing, we shall get in'). I prize our garden wall, so much more ancient than the Legoland rectory it surrounds, as a sign that our exile is not for ever. One day we shall be back where we belong. Perhaps a letter along these lines to the Council will get something done.

Planning for mission was sometimes put on hold by premonitions of mortality.

I was told recently by one more dear to me than any other that I do not always hear what she says. True, I often find the unpalatable inaudible. But to be on the safe side I decided to have my ears looked into. Courtesy of St Luke's Hospital, I was fast-tracked to a high-tec clinic for a series of tests. Apart from assaults on my person by someone apparently from Dyno-Rod, these were unexpectedly agreeable. I was required to lie down in a darkened room with an electrode attached to the top of my head while soothing and vaguely submarine sounds were relayed to me through earphones. I caught myself drifting into a dream that I was back at St James's Piccadilly, meditating to the music of dolphins mating.

The result of the tests was to identify a narrow but deep dip in the upper register of what I can hear in my left ear. My consultant asked me whether I was exposed to loud noises at work. I assured her that ours was a church where the Almighty is worshipped unassisted by youths on drums and thudding loudspeakers. Liberal Christianity is no doubt a very dreadful thing but at least it is quiet. Her next question was more startling. 'Had I ever fired a gun?' I reflected that, while I had shot several church-goers in my time, I had only done so in my heart. But then I remembered my inglorious weeks with the Royal West Kent Regiment when, frequently if inaccurately, I loosed off with a 303 rifle. That apparently was the cause of my problem, even though the injury was inflicted so long ago. I am now wondering whether to sue the Ministry of Defence.

It was convenient to be supposed hard-of-hearing, although I was not so advantaged in this respect as Bishop Russell Barry of Southwell who was known to switch off his hearing aid in a meeting he was finding tedious, even if he was chairing it, and to leave the room with a benedictory gesture to all present. Ears were no problem. Other bits were more of a nuisance.

The clay is beginning to crumble. For the first time I take an interest in what worried the Corinthians – 'With what body do we come?' I read that Origen toyed with the idea that our resurrection bodies will be perfectly spherical. Checking my own inventory of what is known to medical ethics as 'the organic sector', I find that most parts are present, if in some disrepair. The most serious malfunction is a frozen shoulder. This means that I cannot raise my right arm above the horizontal. My GP has referred me to an orthopaedic specialist asking for an early appointment. Treatment is urgent as at present all I can offer the congregation by way of a blessing at the end of Divine service is a Nazi salute.

In the event I had to wait six months for a consultation that lasted six minutes. The consultant burst into the little examination room followed by a scrummage of medical students. At least I suppose that is who they were. There were no introductions, or indeed any other courtesies, and they looked like a bunch of Year 11s on work experience. My discomposure was made worse by the consultant's first question, 'Have you been climbing up the wall?' I wanted to tell him that in my job that is where I am all the time. But apparently the reference is to what they do to frozen shoulders in physiotherapy, an exercise that begins with your being spread-eagled against the side of a house like a Los Angeles dope-peddler about to be body-searched. I was told that it was now too late to put me to sleep and wrench the joint back into place and I was sent away with five yards of bandage, the brand name of which is 'Hospicrepe'. I have no idea what I am supposed to do with it.

Nothing is more disruptive of one's plans for the day than an exploding tooth. I recall from my diary an unplanned visit to the dentist – and an invaluable lesson learned on the way there.

I was early for my appointment and I decided to take a walk to steady my nerves. My dentist's surgery is a stone's throw from Newington Green, a raffish area once a hotbed of dissent. Henry VIII lodged his mistresses in the old Bishop's House on the green. In its shrubberies Daniel Defoe raised his civet cats. John Ball (the Ball of the Ball's Pond Road) ran a pub nearby which promoted 'bull-baiting, drinking and general lechery'. It is a neighbourhood I warm to.

An imposing building caught my eye, a cocktail of architectural conceits. I noticed an inscription emblazoned across a high colonnade, 'Have Faith in God'. With a shock of recognition I knew what I was looking at. This surely was once the headquarters of the China Inland Mission, founded by James Hudson Taylor. Now the building is being gutted. A man in a hard hat told me that it was to become a hostel for university students. Will some of them, I wonder, be curious enough about the place to ask about its history? It is a story to recall now that every good cause has its aggressive fundraiser and churches gladly accept profits from gambling to prop up their buildings. For from here, following Hudson Taylor's example, thousands of missionaries took the Gospel to the back of China's beyond without appealing for a single penny. It almost makes you believe in God.

Sometimes the post contained communications which meant changing plans for the day. Sometimes they simply weakened one's will to live.

Every couple of months the *Church Times* is swollen to twice its size by the inclusion of the latest *Alpha News*. I am thinking of starting a small mutual support group – I shall name it 'Alphaphobics Anonymous' – for those of us, the endemically melancholy and confused, who find this publication depressing. Its relentless chronicle of mounting success is little comfort to those of us whose more modest hope is to muddle through. I hope that Alphaphobics Anonymous gets off the ground but I don't suppose it will. An occasional cyclostyled paper, smudged and misprinted, will chart our feeble and erratic progress. From time to time we shall hold meetings to which few will turn up. Our one publication, *Nostrils – A Neglected Gift?*, will be swiftly remaindered and then pulped. Let me know if you wish to join our unhappy circle. Meanwhile I shall brood on words of Kierkegaard. 'Woe, woe, to the church if it triumphs in this world for then it is the world which will have triumphed and not the church.'

Alphaphobics Anonymous did not last long.

Our secretary, Miss Laceworthy, has defected. The promise of a free chicken salad and the possibility of a smile – all her own – from the Reverend Nicholas Gumbel was too much for her. I have decided what to do. I shall walk off the end of Southend Pier. But perhaps even then there will be no escape. *Underwater Alpha*, I hear, goes from strength to strength.

Plans are resistant to what happens. You don't plan to be burgled, but sooner or later in the inner-city you will be.

While we were away thieves broke in and stole. They bought the dog's silence – indeed her undying devotion – with a couple of biscuits. Then they ransacked the premises. They made off with two computers and a camera. No great loss – the world already has far too many computers and I have yet to take a picture that does not slice off my subject's feet. The really heinous crime was that they turned Rebecca's room over. That, poor Christian that I am, I find hard to forgive. In future I shall add an extra clause to the Prayer Book Commination service, an office I declaim regularly to clear my head of the leaden prose of our modern liturgies –'Cursed is he who that removeth a little girl's piggy-bank'.

Nor, if you're wise, will you plan for a lie-in on your day off.

There is a ring at the door. It is half past eight on Saturday morning. It is my day off and I am still in bed. The only reason I don't stay where I am is the fear that it's the postman with a parcel. If he can't deliver it, it will go back to the Bethnal Green sorting office never to be seen again. I grab the one piece of clothing in reach, an over-the-top silk dressing-gown, and dash downstairs. But it's not the postman. 'Morning,' says the man at the door. 'We're London Loos. We've got twelve toilets for you. On our lorry. Where do you want them?' As so often in my job, I wonder whether I'm hallucinating. Then he explains, apparently unfazed by a vicar looking like Julian Clary with a hangover, 'They're for your concert tonight.' The penny drops. Hackney Singers have hired the church for a concert and the Council won't license you for such an event unless you're equipped to deal with a mass outbreak of dysentery. I tell the chap to take his loos away and to line them up nicely outside the church. Perhaps, if they're still there tomorrow, I'll contrive some liturgical acknowledgement of their presence and utility.

10

My Family and Other Animals

A new incumbent has to keep up the good work begun by his predecessor. On this basis I treat perfectly seriously a letter arriving this week to thank me for having agreed to make the Rectory garden available for the mooring of a condom-shaped balloon for advertising purposes. I am advised that the day-glow orange balloon, promoting the products of 'Deighton Rubberware', will be moored 100 feet above my house. By night it will be illuminated by spotlights guaranteeing its visibility for miles around. I am warned that Health and Safety requirements prohibit the lighting of bonfires in the garden during the mooring period and I am urged to ensure that the lightning conductor from the balloon's pylon is firmly attached to my TV aerial at all times. I try ringing the number on the handsome headed notepaper but it is unobtainable. And then I catch sight of our sixteen-year-old Timothy weeping with suppressed laughter and I remember that, at least for the young, 1 April comes more than once a year.

Clergy often lack self-esteem. They feel guilty that they don't do enough. They own to a sense of failure. Curiously, these same woebegone parsons – such is the complexity of their make-up – may at the same time have a high opinion of themselves. Low self-esteem is sometimes only the flip-side of rampant self-regard. Beneath that same clerical shirt beats a heart well-pleased with itself. We clergy are so vulnerable to self-delusion. We are easily persuaded that we are terribly important. The things we do – pronouncing absolutions and blessings, celebrating sacraments, wearing peculiar clothes in public places, pontificating from pulpits – lead us to imagine that we are a class apart. In truth most of what clergy do is – to borrow Thomas Merton's comment on the role of the sub-deacon at High Mass – 'pretty small potatoes'. It is vital that they are regularly reminded of that fact.

Inflated egos need to be punctured. Some clergy look to their spiritual directors to do this service for them. Others make sure that they have lots of laypeople as friends, men and women doing proper jobs, who can cut them down to size. But married clergy with spouses and families will be stripped of their self-importance every time they go home. Without my family I might have survived as Rector of Hackney. But I dread to think what kind of a self-important monster I would have turned into, had I not shared a home with those less impressed by me than I was. Daughters are the least impressed. They simply find us embarrassing. Our eleven years in Hackney were the years our daughter was growing up. My diary has several snapshots of her.

> To pass the time on our morning walk to school Rebecca and I play a game. We each guess how many dogs and how many cats we are going to see. Whichever of us estimates the more accurately is the winner. But today Beccy tells me that she is bored with this game. 'I'm going to count old ladies instead,' she announces. I ask her how you tell an old lady from a young lady. 'Old ladies have crinkly hair and little wrinkly faces,' she says. So, dear woman reader, if on your lawful occasions out and about in Hackney you meet a child who gravely contemplates you and then says decisively, 'Twenty-seven', you will know, alas, that she is not guessing your age.

> Our daughter, still only seven, went on one of the 'Forest School Camps' this summer. She had a fantastic fortnight on a farm high in the Yorkshire dales. The Forest School Camps preserve something of the spirit of the original and now long defunct Forest School, a back-to-nature establishment run by a group of cranky visionaries on a property deep in the New Forest named – I do not lie – 'Sandy Balls'. Here children danced under the trees, bathed in the altogether, and lived off a diet of herrings and compressed dates. The school was the idea of Ernest Westlake, a Quaker botanist in love with the simple life

who founded the Order of Woodcraft Chivalry from which in due course there seceded the yet more dotty Kibbo Kift Kindred. Westlake believed that children need to recapitulate the earlier stages of the evolutionary process. 'The man who when young has never been a monkey or a mole,' he said, 'will never in his prime make a great citizen'. The Forest School Camps today are not in the least loopy and my wife and I have nothing but praise for an organisation which looked after our daughter well, affirmed her childhood, and gave her a wonderful time.

On our family holiday we found ourselves together in a hotel room properly fitted-out with tea-making facilities, television, and a Gideon Bible. There being nothing to her taste on the telly, our Rebecca decided to re-read the Bible. She had already read a children's Bible from cover to cover. Now it was time for a grown-up version. She ground to a halt at Genesis chapter 2, verse 2. 'It's saying the same thing twice,' she protested. Which indeed it is. I tried to explain to her how the parallelism of Hebrew poetry works, how a concept is conveyed by the interplay of complementary expressions, never as a single proposition. Thus the meaning is never in the lines, but always between the lines so that scriptural 'truth', contrary to all that I claimed in my conservative youth, is not to be found in what 'the Bible says' but in what it does not say, not in the words but in the spaces between them. At which point I realised that this was a seriously weird conversation to be having with one's twelve-year-old on holiday and changed the subject.

I am sitting in the café at the Marble Arch ice rink. It is the end of term and Rebecca is on the ice with three of her teenage friends. They are not expert skaters but they move with a grace rarely won in later years. I think of a children's classic, Helen Cresswell's *A Game of Catch*, the story of Kate who goes skating on the castle lake. There is the faint sound of laughter in the mist. Furrows appear mysteriously before her in the ice, 'turning, wheeling, curving . . . doubling back, elusive as smoke'. These are the tracks of children who had lived in the castle centuries before, children who also skated on this frozen lake. Was Kate seeing these tracks? Or was she imagining them? (Joe, the old caretaker of the castle, will say to her 'there ain't all that much difference'). I emerge from this reverie to see that my daughter is being carried from the ice on a stretcher and I am briefly sick with fear. Although it is soon clear that she is not badly hurt, a drama has begun that must now run its course. In the ambulance the medics take a pair of scissors to her expensive jeans to examine the injured knee. At the hospital A. and E. the 'triage' process swings into action. Is our Beccy an emergency or can she wait? She can wait – and so she does and so do we. But not so long that the subsequent 'sleep-over' is sabotaged. There's still time for a take-away, a soppy video, and wicked gossip deep into the night.

Rebecca is our youngest, but she has older siblings now wedded and with their own children. Rebecca had her part to play, as I did, in one of those weddings.

I announced my text: 'Miwosht wszystko znosi' 'Love bears all things'. The occasion was my step-son Oliver's wedding to his gentle Polish bride, Kasia, in the church of St George's, Chichester. My clumsy effort to quote St Paul in Polish was appreciated by the bride's family. It was matrimony at its most magical. The bridegroom had spent the previous week in our garage making his bride a pair of shoes for the wedding. As in a fairy tale, they were fashioned from some fabulous stuff, lighter than gossamer but stronger than steel. Beneath the drifting cloud of her dress the bride's enchanted shoes left no print on the carpet of rose petals strewed before her by the youngest bridesmaid, our own Rebecca. Since this was an occasion for dressing-up I wore a cope – for only the second time in my thirty years as a priest. It was a bitterly cold day and I was very glad of it. So were my wife and daughter when, for the photographs, I wrapped them in its ample folds. 'Miwosht wszystko znosi' 'Love bears all things'. The words have long haunted me. They are the baptised rendering of Hamlet's 'the readiness is all'. There is more that we must suffer than ever we can change. It is our most grievous burden but, as I pray that Oliver and Kasia will discover, 'under the Mercy' it is also our greatest benediction.

'Love bears all things' – even the Church of England. Later that same wedding day I absented myself from the revels and slipped into Chichester Cathedral for the tail-end of Choral Evensong. I sat at the back of an empty nave. Far away beyond the screen a bishop was reading from the Bible. 'Women should be silent in the churches. For they are not permitted to speak, but should be subordinate as the law says. If there is anything they desire to know let them ask their husbands at home. For it is shameful for a woman to speak in church.' What would the intelligent young couple I had just married have made of that, I wondered? What must they think of a church which continues to authorise the unloading of toxic waste from its lecterns? Usually I find such moments comic. That night I was overwhelmed by a deep foreboding for my church. In that vast deserted house, for all its beauty, for all the aching loveliness of a sublime *Nunc Dimittis*, I felt myself as if in the bowels of some huge abandoned hulk drifting towards shipwreck.

Family weddings were followed by family baptisms.

Two of our grandchildren, Alex and Lola, have recently been baptised. Alex was baptised at a 'children's mass'. The children sat up straight and behaved themselves, for this was in Poland not Hackney. A little girl near the front was dressed exactly like the demure subject of John Everett Millais's 'My First Sermon'. The service was striking for its absence of theatre. There is no need to strive for effect in a society which has yet to wonder whether any of this is really necessary. Alex received the sacrament with the same look of quizzical amusement which he invariably turns on this absurd world he has lately entered.

I baptised Lola – at the kind invitation of Father Andrew Davis – during Mass at the church of Christ the Saviour, Ealing. Lola voiced a strong protest. I like it when babies cry at the font. It is as if their innate spiritual insight has allowed them a glimpse of what they are being let in for. As Father Andrew pointed out in his lively children's talk – in which he deftly demonstrated the proper use of the aspergillium – 'You're baptised for ever.'

The only inhabitants of the rectory who shared my exalted estimate of myself were our dog and our cats – and of course the cats were only flattering me. Our dog Blue was very dear to us, all the more so that she was disabled by epilepsy. Blue was a Hungarian Vizla. She reminded me of my first rural dean, huge of rump and heart, a lover of cake, everywhere at once and wanting everyone to be happy but far too dominating in the drawing room. The idea was that she would make me take some exercise and provide pastoral openings. Certainly she got me out and about, but I am less sure how much of an asset she proved in my ministry. The bereaved do not always want their faces licked. But what she did do was to teach me charity. Our dog Blue bore all things, believed all things, hoped all things, endured all things. I kept trying to get her not to jump up, because I was sure that one day she would be very near the throne.

One morning a curious communication landed on the doormat. It was written on the back of an envelope. 'Please excuse my for-wardness,' my anonymous correspondent wrote. 'I have a *serious* problem. I'm very concerned about your dog. I believe her name is "Blue". I met her once and could see she is *mentally ill*.' And so it went on. It was not written in green ink, but there was much recourse to upper-case lettering and double underlining. My correspondent said that 'God would be extremely happy' if Blue were in a better home and that she (why did I assume the writer was female?) would be willing to provide one. Warming to her theme, she shouted, 'ALL ANIMALS ARE PERFECT. It is us who are the real evil.' So if our dog was bonkers it was all our fault. I agree that Blue was far off her trolley. But I reject the allegation that we'd driven her mad. It was the other way round. The bishop came to visit us. Blue ate his lunch. One night I caught her helping herself to my supper. Reaching out to drag her from the table, I managed to dislodge the crown from one of my front teeth. Repairs cost three hundred pounds.

Dear Blue – how we miss you, now you are gone! I wrote of her passing in my diary.

Our daft dog 'Blue' is dead. Just before dawn on Advent Sunday she had an epileptic fit, staggered into the pond in our garden, and drowned. We were more upset than I would have believed possible. Later that morning I was preaching at the family service. I gave a talk peppered with the seasonal punch-line, 'We've not seen the last of Jesus'. I said – as I had planned – 'We've not seen the last of those we've loved and lost.' But then I strayed from my script. By some impulse I added, 'We've not seen the last of Blue.' Nobody seemed startled by this latest sign of the Rector losing his marbles. Indeed my colleague conducting the service included Blue in his thanksgiving for the 'faithful departed'. To which prayer all who knew our beloved Blue, who defined fidelity, will add their 'Amen'. May she rest in peace and rise in glory.

We had three cats in our time in Hackney, all Burmese. Parker, who was very beautiful, was stolen. Bow-Bell is still with us, reconciled at last to living somewhere far less exciting than Hackney. Because Bow-Bell is of noble blood we decided to breed from her. We made arrangements to introduce her to a gentleman of the same breed. The cattery where the assignation took place was a remote fog-bound bungalow deep in the Fens. We drove between the haunted bogs and drains of East Anglia to be greeted at our journey's end by banshee cries, not it transpired of the long-drowned, but of scores of Burmese cats wailing for their meat and demon lovers. The brute to whom our gentle Bow-Bell was presented was the solitary occupant of an overheated caravan at the bottom of the garden. This ancient, malevolent, and clearly exhausted stud was crouched on a decomposing sofa in front of a television watching the racing from Lingfield. He only performed, the proprietor told us, with the television on. We left the two cats together on the sofa, and, rather ashamed of ourselves, drove back to Hackney. In the event the raddled old beast failed to oblige and a week later we collected our slighted little one and brought her home. She promptly ran off and arranged a more satisfactory meeting with the tom next door. Perhaps he was a Cheshire – certainly Bow-Bell now has a smile on her face.

Our third Burmese, Kipling, lived out his days and ended his days in Hackney. I wrote of him in my diary:

> One of Kipling's thirty-two great-great-great-great-grandparents was Pussinboots Burmaboy. I refer not to Rudyard Kipling but to our cat Kipling who died a few days ago. He was of proud and ancient lineage. We have the resounding names of the other thirty-one great-great-great-great grandparents, Braeside Moonbeam, Muscadin Apollo, Artemis Lady Emma, and the rest. Kipling slept in a basket by my desk. I found him curled up there for his longer sleep just before going across to the church to take a mid-week communion service. At the altar, when I came to 'bring us with [N and] all the saints to feast at your table in heaven', I named Kipling under my breath. And why not? Christopher Smart's cat Jeoffrey was 'a servant of the living God' and so was my cat Kipling. We buried Kipling next to our Zen garden. Cats have much in common with the Zen masters. Unlike dogs and clergy, they are not at the mercy of the contingent and transient.

Blue and Kipling were both given Christian burial and both rest in our rectory garden. I do not know whether animals have souls, but they suffer as much pain as we do and inflict far less evil. They also give us great joy. Hackney people love their animals. I suspect that there are proportionately more cats and dogs per head of population in Hackney than up the road in swanky Islington. Ministry to those in the inner-city has to be inclusive enough to affirm and honour the animals with which many of them share their family lives and their limited resources. I never actually baptized anyone's pet. That was not because I feared further attention from the thought police. I did not baptize animals because I believe in their original innocence.

11

Out of Hackney

'I saw eternity the other night' – or at least I glimpsed it one morning in August. We were on holiday, as we are each year, in a hidden valley of the Usk. It was Henry Vaughan, born beneath the Brecons, who made this river his own. Vaughan, whose shade still haunts the Usk – 'Dear stream! Dear bank, where often I have sat and pleased my pensive eye' – saw eternity there most nights. He called a volume of his poems 'Olor Iscanus' – 'The Swan of the Usk'. No other poet so sweetly held together the love of this world and of 'the country far beyond the stars'. To delight in the Usk and to long for 'the river, the streams whereof shall make glad the city of God' was, for Vaughan, ultimately the same affection. For him the river, both the Usk and the river of one's days, is 'a quickness which my God hath kissed'. Both have their source in the 'sea of light' to which they both return. I sat by the Usk at dawn that August morning and, for a moment, I knew that it was so.

The secret of staying in love with your parish is to get out of it regularly. There is more to this requirement than the obvious need to take a holiday from time to time, as we did year by year on the banks of the Usk, and to recoup by making a regular retreat. The relationship of priest and people is an intense one. Most clergy are wedded to their parishes. Such a marriage will work – as will the relationship of husband and wife – only so long as both partners have their own space. The incumbent and the parish need sometimes to leave each other alone. The parson who never goes anywhere eventually goes do-lally. The church is blessed by its eccentric clergy but not by its unhinged clergy. But the most compelling reason for a parish priest to clear out of his or her parish

127

periodically is not psychological but theological. The problem with parochial ministry is just that, that it is *parochial*, that it is confined to a particular grid of streets and houses or of fields and farms. Christianity, like other accounts of the human condition, knows no such frontiers. It is a world faith. 'For God so loved the cosmos ...' my Bible says. If my faith takes no account of the world beyond my parish, that faith will be diminished and distorted. Hackney is home to the world and its wife, but it still affords only a partial view of the kingdom of God. To reduce one's horizons to the boundaries of one neighbourhood – even a neighbourhood as diverse as Hackney – would be to invite spiritual sclerosis.

Bishops, to be fair to them, see the need for their clergy to get out more. For that reason they arrange the occasional conference for them. Such events are supposed to extend our horizons. A diocesan conference in 2001 did so, but – as I recall from my diary – in a way no one would have wished.

> The clergy of the East End and the City are rounded up for a conference every three years. This year (2001) we convened at St Catherine's College, Oxford. (St Cat's was designed by a modern architect who believed in transparency. Instead of windows each room has a wall of glass. Tourists could inspect a succession of vicars at – amongst other things – their devotions.) The theme was 'Urban ministry at a time of change'. I have been going to conferences for forty years. I have forgotten absolutely everything about all of them except that each one was, we were told, 'at a time of change'. I would have preferred a conference entitled 'Ministry when things are much the same as this time last week'. Alas, in the event over those three days the world was changed most cruelly. The session on the morning of Tuesday 11 September – before the towers fell – was on 'The Changing Church'. A with-it bishop used power-point to project blueprints of a brave new church on to a vast screen. Old hands, knowing that none of this would be in their lifetime, checked their programmes to see if the bar was open before lunch.
>
> I wondered why nothing was said – to a body of Londoners of all people – about the church and other faith communities. The absurd-

ity of such isolationism was brought home to me a little later in the day. I had escaped to the Ashmolean Museum. In the gallery of Eastern Art I paused before a superb thirteenth-century carving of a seated Boddhisatva. The description below quoted a text from the *Varjradhavaja Sutra*: 'I take upon myself the burden of all suffering'. There are stories other than our own that tell of one who carried our sorrows and that bid us bear each other's burdens. A church which ignores that fact, however radically restructured, shows that all it really cares about is its own identity and survival. Returning to Cats, I ran into Liz Carmichael, Chaplain of St John's College and honoured veteran of the struggle for a just South Africa. The burden she was bearing just then was an agitated young man who had button-holed her. As I joined them he was talking wildly about aeroplanes flying into skyscrapers. Within the hour I was heading fearfully home, fearful for my wife working the other side of the Atlantic, fearful for my church which will not allow that others share its gospel, fearful for my beautiful broken world.

Four years later the East End clergy were bussed and shipped to France.

Why France? Because it was cheaper and there was less chance of slackers sloping off. We met in a frowning four-square pile, formerly a seminary and an architectural proclamation of the austere religion once taught there. *Il n'y avait pas de fauteuils*. The plan of the place indicated that there was a television room somewhere. I thought I'd found it until I realised that I was contemplating a microwave. Cells were allocated with exquisite tact. Incumbents had en-suite showers. Area Deans and Prebendaries had baths. The lower orders – curates and the like – were obliged to tread endless dimly-lit corridors to attend to their ablutions. (The talk at table was that the most highly elevated had their beds made.)

The consensus of the conference was that those we serve seek in us confidence and conviction. Why am I uneasy about so evident a conclusion? No doubt because my theology, like my dress-sense, is stuck in the sixties. My problem – my 'baggage' in the conference vernacular – is that I am oversensitive about those put off by strident claims

about what we can never know for sure. I am troubled by the slow geo-
logical shift in the focus of our church's attention over the last forty
years from questions of meaning and truth to methods of management and marketing. But I still headed home on a high. We were
well-nourished – by weighty presentations, by worship which
acknowledged our woes as well as our joys, and by first-rate French
cooking. Above all there were the saints and the butterflies. The
clergy round here are a merry bunch, Tiggers to my Eeyore. Bishop
Roy Williamson's three-minute reflections at evening prayer were living water. And in the seminary grounds there was an orchard of apple
trees. Butterflies, gorged on the cidrous windfalls, danced giddily in
the autumn sunshine. They know. Perhaps one day I will too.

Relaxed and informal as they are, conferences called by those in
authority are never altogether free of a certain constraint. Younger
clergy with careers to cultivate worry whether anyone will notice if
they miss the daily offices. They wonder whether they dare say what
they really think. It is a matter of some consequence whom you sit
next to at lunch. No such inhibitions affected any of the annual
conferences of the Modern Churchpeople's Union I used to attend.
I recalled one memorable MCU conference in my diary.

To a standing ovation Bishop Spong was bundled off the platform,
out through the fire exit and into the car ready to race him to his next
engagement. It was the high moment in the Centenary conference of
the Modern Churchpeople's Union. I could not prophesy my way
out of a paper bag, but I predict that this year's assembly will turn out
to be as seminal as the famous 1921 Girton conference, an event that
so outraged the thought-police that before you could say John
Robinson they'd set up the Commission on Doctrine in the Church
of England. This latest conference is likely to prove far too powerful
to be defused by any such manoeuvre. I dare to believe that it will be
remembered as the hour in English church history when liberalism at
last regained its nerve, when it ceased to be so obsessively polite,
when it awoke to the fact that it too has a gospel to proclaim. How
simple it all really is! Liberalism is a matter of disposition not doc-

trine, the readiness – to quote the theme of our conference – 'to think the unthinkable'. It is the willingness to change one's mind, in a word to 'repent'. Whether you are a fisherman in Galilee or a stockbroker attending St Helen's Bishopsgate you have to be a liberal to become a Christian in the first place. Every convert is a Jack Spong. What a peculiar religion it would be if, having turned the giddiest intellectual somersault of your life, you then were required to cross the floor of the church to spend the rest of your days denouncing that very openness to new truth without which you would never have given the tall tale of Jesus a second thought!

Hackney is a scene of social deprivation and simmering conflict. So too is Sri Lanka. I had travelled to that beautiful but afflicted island several times in earlier years. Twenty years ago I was involved in establishing the Kandy Children's Centre, a refuge for some of the many 'street children' of Kandy. On one of those early visits I met a couple who were to prove a blessing to us. Reggie and Audrey Ebenezer were a great support when we adopted a Sri Lankan child as our daughter. They continue to be an inspiration as I reflect on the role and cost of the Christian ministry in communities nearer home that are ill-disposed to one another. While in Hackney we went back to Sri Lanka so that our Rebecca could see where she was born. It was also a chance to see Reggie and Audrey again.

Supper with Reggie and Audrey Ebenezer in the fabled but faded splendour of the Galle Face Hotel, Colombo. A moist-eyed ancient, conducting us through its cavernous public rooms, recalls its past glory. Tonight the only movement across the sprung floor of its vast ballroom is the measured tread of a lone cockroach. Our guests, preoccupied with Sri Lanka's contemporary afflictions, are less nostalgic. Reggie's testimony is striking. Twenty years ago – at that time he was a minister of the Dutch Reformed Church – his car stalled on a level-crossing and was struck by a train. He survived, despite being shunted a hundred yards down the track. He drily observes, 'I think God was telling me something.' He abandoned his pastorate and – there is the Johannine precedent – went out of 'the temple' to embrace a suffering humanity. Today he and Audrey regularly travel deep into the war-torn zones of northern Sri Lanka in a van loaded with Bibles, tooth-paste, health-care manuals, bicycle inner-tubes, sugar, hymn-books, and concrete (for pit latrines). This fearless couple, who surrounded and sustained us with their love and prayers as we adopted our Rebecca Sujani, are very dear to us.

From Colombo we went to visit the home of another family who for many years have served some of Sri Lanka's neediest children. That was the occasion too, as I noted at the time, of being brought painfully down to earth.

The Paynter Homes were founded in the days of the Raj to care for children born as a result of recreational activities of British Army officers in and around the cool hill station of Nuwara Eliya. Today the Homes still look after unwanted children, no less effectively now that they have something of the air of a Victorian mission station. We are greeted by 'Auntie' Val Paynter, the widow of the founder of the Homes and a fount of anecdote about her remarkable family. A tiny vibrant figure, she seats us by the fire – a welcome blaze for the chilling monsoon rains have come early this year – and shares her memories with us, recollections of an age and of a pattern of missionary endeavour that now seem infinitely remote. Reminders of the most gifted member of the Paynter dynasty are all about us, for the walls of the sitting-room are crowded with some of the surviving canvases of her brother-in-law, David Paynter. David Paynter was perhaps the greatest artist of the twentieth century to have worked in the Indian sub-continent. Who today has heard of him? Who else comes through these bitter rains to view his work, reaching at last this remote house where the track ends beneath a sodden forest? Who else pauses before the picture hanging above the fireplace, entitled 'The Blind Evangelist', and finds they are close to tears?

On leaving the Paynter Homes I slip on the treacherous laterite and crack my skull. But then Sri Lanka is an island on which I have always had some difficulty in remaining vertical. I recall an earlier visit. I had been lecturing at the Pilimatalawa Theological College. Many of the students were wearing white for mourning. Their choice of dress, I

gathered, was not because my appearance was such a ghastly intima-
tion of our mortality. One of their lecturers, and the most popular,
had just been given the heave-ho for, allegedly, teaching heresy and
this was their protest. It was an altogether depressing evening, its
melancholy for me not assuaged when in my haste to make a quick
get-away I fell into an irrigation ditch.

One of the largest communities in Hackney is the Vietnamese. The
local Vietnamese restaurants are superb. Less benign is the market
in pirated DVDs which the Vietnamese control. A brilliantly gifted
Vietnamese student was a guest in our Rectory for some weeks. She
came to church once or twice, but was understandably baffled by
what was going on. I was embarrassed, as so often I have been, by
the oddity of what we do in church. In Vietnam itself Christianity
is perceived – if noticed at all – as Western and alien. A generation
after America's catastrophic involvement in that country, the
communist government, while officially granting religious freedom, polices religious activity closely. However, devotion to the
memory of the architect of modern Vietnam, with all its quasi-
religious fervour, is not discouraged. A visit to our guest's home-
land helped me understand our Vietnamese neighbours better.

I observed Low Sunday by inspecting Ho Chi Minh's corpse. With
ten thousand others I queued to troop through the huge marble
mausoleum where his embalmed remains lie. His margarine features
express grim satisfaction. Certainly the old warrior has much to be
satisfied about. He has every reason to be proud of these pilgrims to
his resting-place, these whose spirit the napalm could not quench.
Ho's mausoleum is open to criticism. 'The grandiose building,' says
my Rough Guide, 'seems sadly at odds with a simple unassuming
man'. Those are my sentiments about Hackney Parish Church and
Jesus. Ho Chi Minh said of Jesus, Confucius and Marx, 'If they were
grouped together they would live in harmony like close friends'. The
present circumstances of Jesus of Nazareth, if our creeds are to be
believed, do not preclude the possibility of such a meeting. I like to
think that the three of them are now getting on famously.

The prospect of Jesus, Confucius and Marx making peace with one another may seem far off, even absurd, but it is an altogether more exciting vision and infinitely more worthwhile pursuing, than that of papering over the divisions of Christendom. I reflect sadly that there is so much that impedes the realization of large visions, above all the clamorous demands of the unspeakably trivial. No doubt Confucius had wise things to say about our lamentable preoccupation with the penultimate. The Buddha certainly did.

> Our trip to Vietnam allows a brief detour to neighbouring Cambodia and to Angkor Wat. Angkor Wat, we are told, is 'the biggest religious monument in the world'. (Previously I had thought that that distinction belonged to someone we have met before, my first Rural Dean.) The roots of the great fever trees still embrace the colossal stones they dislodged when the forest returned, for centuries veiling these overwhelming structures from human sight. Deep in one of the labyrinthine temples, a city in itself, we stumble on a tiny Buddhist shrine. Two elderly nuns tend this hidden sanctuary, reclaiming its holiness. I light a stick of incense, pause for a moment in reflection on suffering and the end of suffering, leave a dollar in a dish, and reluctantly return to the world of appearances. It is a gesture, merely. The longing is not for nirvana, not this time round at least, but simply for a measure of detachment, for sufficient 'right mindfulness' to be less at the mercy of the contingent and absurd.

Because a whole generation of Cambodian intellectuals was slaughtered in the killing fields – the few that escaped fleeing to the ends of the earth – there are far too few scholars researching the phenomenal wealth of Khmer culture. I cannot explain why that thought should still have worried me once we were home in Hackney again, but worry me it did. It was the thought on my mind, one morning soon after we were back, when the doorbell rang.

> I answer the door and meet a young man with a problem. 'A squirrel has fallen out of a tree in your churchyard,' he tells me. 'It's

wounded, bleeding. My girl-friend is nursing it. I need to contact the RSPCA.' His accent is French. Clearly my ordination vows commit me to a ministry to wounded squirrels, so I let him use my phone. The emergency services having been summoned, the young man collects his breath and introduces himself. His name is Philippe and his home is Cambodia where he is the Director of the Institute of Khmer Studies. Suddenly the universe tilts. This world is not as safe as we like to think.

Buddhists know that nothing lasts. Any good ruin testifies to the same truth.

We spend our post-Easter break with friends who are about to open a factory just outside Carthage for the mass production of air-bags. (I toy briefly with the idea of composing an edifying vignette on the making of air-bags and the unmaking of Carthage, on our twin compulsions to save life and to destroy it. But I decide it is much too hot.) We are shown round the baking ruins of Carthage by a brilliant woman who at other times has the most ghastly job imaginable. She gives conducted tours of the site to parties disgorged at dawn from Mediterranean cruise-liners. These forlorn souls are often uncertain as to which continent they're in. She tells us a cautionary tale. Her route round the ruins usually ends at the impressive remains of the public baths. Recently, having explained at length the importance of such facilities to the Romans and the manner of their ablutions, she invited questions. Someone queried, 'Was all this damage done in the first world-war or the second?' So surely one day, perhaps far nearer than we think, bemused travellers will survey with blank incomprehension the relics of the ecclesiastical institutions and edifices we vainly strive to maintain. *Delenda est Carthago.*

Let it not be supposed that as Rector of Hackney I could afford to travel to Sri Lanka, the Far East, or North Africa very often. Most excursions were much less extended, but they too had their moments, as my diary reminds me.

Pat and I celebrate our tenth wedding anniversary by stealing a week-end in Paris. The nice family who run the shop ('Best for Less') at the bottom of our drive ask us to bring back a *gateau de riz* for them. We are not sure what that is. Perhaps it is the confection which inspired the building of the church of the Sacré-Cœur, clearly the concoction of an architect too fond of cake. We are there for Mass, where a softly-spoken celebrant is upstaged by the strapping nun conducting the singing. She flaps her arms with much abandon, imperilling the security of her wimple.

Round the Louvre at the double. The Mona Lisa ('hers is the head upon which all the ends of the world are come and the eyelids are a little weary') smiles enigmatically on the tourists jostling to be pho-tographed in front of her. She too comes to us, like another famously inscrutable character, 'as one unknown'. Many have sought to solve the mystery of her identity. The suggestion which I find most attrac-tive is that the Mona Lisa is in fact the daughter of a Woking plumber. This thesis is argued, not in a learned article in *The Journal of Renaissance Studies*, but in a play I once saw at the Yvonne Arnaud Theatre in Guildford. The plumber with his wife and daughter are on holiday in Florence. They are unaware that their hotel was once the home of Leonardo da Vinci. Nor does the daughter appreciate that there is 'a singularity' in her en-suite bathroom through which she may travel in time. While taking a shower, she suddenly finds herself in the artist's studio five hundred years ago. Leonardo falls in love with her, paints the picture of her we all know so well, and proposes to her. I've forgotten most of this pot-boiler, though one remark of the girl's mother does come back to me. 'I wonder what they'll say in Woking when word gets round that I'm Leonardo da Vinci's mother-in-law.'

There is just time to see a work to which I lost my heart when young and which has haunted my imagination ever since. It is the loveliest tapestry on earth, the sequence of fifteenth-century panels known as 'The Lady and the Unicorn' in the Cluny Museum. The kneeling unicorn looks with adoration on his mistress. She touches him but very sadly, absorbed, it seems, in her own sorrows. Again we do not know who she is. Drained of her mystery, her sway over us would be gone. Like the Mona Lisa, like Jesus.

If you are an inner-city parson there are two things you must do to stay sane. First, you need to get away often enough to gain the distance necessary to see your ministry in perspective. Secondly – this is more difficult, but essential – you must somehow maintain that distance inwardly once you are back in your parish. By keeping that 'inner distance' you do not disengage from what you are doing, but you may avoid – or at least postpone – your nervous breakdown. A Christian commentator who understood the importance of ironic detachment was Soren Kierkegaard. When from time to time I fell out with my betters, the thought of Kierkegaard was a great comfort. A brief visit to Copenhagen allowed me to honour his memory.

A cold grey morning in Copenhagen. (My wife is giving a lecture at the university and I have briefly joined her.) Apart from a melancholy jogger who has paused to feel his pulse – perhaps to ascertain whether he is still alive – I have the cemetery to myself. Here beneath three sad cypresses Kierkegaard lies buried. I place some flowers on his grave. I think of the brouhaha at Kierkegaard's burial, of that last 'attack on Christendom' launched over his corpse. A church dignitary, we are told, had read the authorised words of committal when, just as the coffin was being lowered into the ground, a young man in the crowd protested. He denounced the establishment's hypocrisy in burying its fiercest critic as one of its own. He yelled out Kierkegaard's own words, 'Whoever does not take part in the official worship of God has one less sin to confess.' A great rumpus broke out around the grave. But the day was cold and eventually everyone drifted away. Except for the gravediggers, whose observations on these events are unrecorded.

Clergy are advised to take a day off a week. As so much of their work these days is managerial rather than ministerial, secular rather than spiritual, there is a case for saying that they should have the equivalent of the weekend enjoyed by everyone else. Many clergy think so and give themselves a 'midweek weekend', although they don't tell anyone for fear of being thought lazy or uncommitted. I tried to take Saturday as a day off, but I did not feel that I had to make excuses if occasionally I was 'out of the office' for a weekday as well. The important thing was to be somewhere else, Henley, for example, or Ely.

They would not let me in because I was improperly dressed. I wondered whether to plead the solemnity of my orders and the dignity of my office. I had a friend with me, an Emeritus Canon Theologian of a great cathedral and a moral philosopher of international eminence. Like Abraham interceding for the lost of Sodom, he sought to persuade the gatekeepers to let me pass. Their refusal was adamantine. I was told to depart to my own place. All this was not some dreadful night vision of my doom on the last day. It happened in broad daylight at the gate of the Stewards' Enclosure at the Henley Regatta, a hallowed acre as unlike Hackney as anywhere on earth. (Ask me what I was doing at Henley on my day off and I shall reminisce movingly, if mendaciously, about the Balliol boat of '62.) Without a tie I was a pariah. My companion swiftly fashioned a fetching cravat from a blue paper napkin he had about his person and stuck it in my shirt. But the gate – 'with dreadful faces thronged and fiery arms'– remained unpassable. I stole a glance within where the elect, gorgeously and correctly apparelled, went about their high business. 'Which things, when I had seen, I wished myself among them.' Then I turned away. 'Some natural tears I dropped, but wiped them soon'. After all, though outside is 'all abyss', outside is where I belong.

A moment out of time in the company of four clergymen of the old school high above the Octagon of Ely Cathedral. We were all students together at Ridley Hall in its latitudinarian days. Each year we reunite to wine and dine together, to exchange scurrilous gossip, and to lament the passing of those arcadian days when training for the ministry was not the dreadfully intense business it now is. It is the loveliest day of the year. The little city of Ely, curled round the Cathedral, sleeps in the sun. Beyond the bungaloid suburbs and the ring-road, the fens to the far horizon are fields of praise. Immediately beneath us is the Bishop's croquet lawn and vegetable garden. A stooped figure is rooting among the tubers. From this height and elevation it is impossible to tell whether it is His Lordship.

Apart from a figure in blue overalls, busy behind a buttress, we have this high and holy place to ourselves. 'Don't mind me,' he says. 'I live here.' The Dean tells us that he is the pigeon man, charged to make war on those creatures which, unlike their unfallen cousins the doves, are enemies to the house of God. Speaking of birds in high places, the Dean reminds us of how they used to commemorate his predecessor Dean Peacock who restored the Octagon in the nineteenth century. Each year on the first holy day in April live peacocks were released from the Octagon into the nave of the cathedral while the choir below sang the Hallelujah Chorus. Alas, the custom, like so much of charming inconsequence in our Church, has been discontinued. One of our company is the Chairman of the English Clergy Association. In recognition that this is a holy place and a holy time, he has switched off both his mobile phones. He has much of the Prayer Book Psalter by heart, as well as many obscure deliverances of Anglican canon law. Today is the thirtieth morning and he declaims to the cloudless skies, 'Happy are the people that are in such a case: yea, blessed are the people who have the Lord for their God.' Amen, I say, Amen.

Occasionally I was called to a pulpit or platform away from Hackney. Such away-fixtures are good for a cleric. You choose your words more carefully when talking to those you have not met before. I noted some of these outings in my diary.

Cuddesdon, always far ahead of the field, arranges a short course each summer for incumbents about to employ a curate. This year my curate Jonathan and I were invited to take part. In turn we talked about a relationship which, if it works as well as ours does, is a great boon to all parties, but if it goes wrong leaves much blood on the vestry carpet. I shared my memories of the two men from whom I learned so much when serving my title, the saintly George Sandfield who taught me that there is indeed a country far beyond the stars and dear Basil Brown who taught me not to flap. Curates come to their parishes with high ideals. The incumbent's task is ease them gently back to earth, to induct them into the realities of parochial ministry where so often at the day's end one has to settle for the second-best, the job half-done, the compromise with the wicked world wedded and bedded by an established church. As for those high ideals, the incumbent can only pray that the parish does not prove an unholy sepulchre where they are bound and buried. Don't become cynical, Jonathan. Not just yet.

I enjoyed a recent event at Norwich cathedral. My pleasure in the programme – a lecture in the south transept on George MacDonald, Choral Evensong, wine and canapés in the Cloisters – was marred only by the fact that I was giving the lecture. I arrived early enough to sit quietly in the nave to collect my thoughts and to pray the prayer of the ill-prepared. There were few visitors that afternoon and the silence of the great building was balm in Gilead. The peace of God enfolded me. Until, that is, the explosion. Someone was addressing me through a loudspeaker six inches from my left ear. The sound level was adjusted so as to be audible by the hard-of-hearing through- out the diocese. 'This is the Cathedral Chaplain. I invite you to join me now in a short prayer'. A kind suggestion which, due to cardiac arrest, I was unable to take up.

When I told the family that I'd been asked to talk to the Clore Fellows about leadership there was stifled laughter. (My family forgets that I too have been a leader of men. On one occasion in my army days I found myself in sole command of six soldiers on a train journey from Uckfield to Harwich.) The Clore Fellows are leaders in 'the cultural sector'. They run theatres, orchestras, art-galleries and the like and the fellowship programme is designed to boost their leadership skills. The dozen or so Fellows I met at the Whitechapel Gallery were as brilliant a group of creative people as you would ever be likely to find all in one room at one time. I talked to them – 'sailing to Byzantium' – about the governance of the Church of England. Chatham House Rules applied, so I'm not free to disclose what was said. I hope it doesn't break those rules to mention that the Fellows were surprised to learn that my appointment as Rector of Hackney had to be approved by the Rear-Commodore of the Royal Yacht Squadron.

I am here in France to conduct a conference for the Anglican church in Strasbourg. Many attending hold down high-powered jobs with the Council of Europe. We meet in *La Maison de l'Eglise*, a religious house high in the Vosges. The theme for our weekend is the story of Jonah. Jonah is about the most neglected book in the Bible. Why, I wonder? Perhaps it is because it contains so many hot potatoes. Prayer to pagan gods is not called in question; Yahweh 'repents of the evil' he had planned to do; animals, it seems, have souls. Perhaps it is because we too are an evil and adulterous generation seeking for a sign and we resent the fact that 'the sign of Jonah' is the only one we shall get. Perhaps a tale that tells of a God who can whistle up a wind and a whale, a caterpillar and a castor-oil plant, but who cannot make Jonah love his enemies challenges our settled assumptions about divine omnipotence. Perhaps in a Christian culture terrified of question-marks we shy away from the only book in the Bible to end with one. Perhaps it is our primal fear of the bowels of Leviathan. Not that, fugitives that we all are, there is any escaping those gently smiling jaws. 'The whale and the prophet will soon come around and meet again in their wanderings,' writes Thomas Merton, 'and once again the whale will swallow the prophet'.

I believe that Hackney benefited from the fact that I was not always there. I hope that it was for the good of the parish that, thanks to a kindly diocese, I was granted a sabbatical – or 'study leave' as now it must be called. I used those months to pursue a question that had dogged me for years. My beloved George MacDonald believed in God and in his many novels he spoke of him with eloquence. Yet in his fantasy and fairy tales, works far profounder and spiritually more persuasive than his fiction, he does not talk about God at all. My question was this – does spirituality require the language of a religious tradition? George MacDonald made me wonder. That was the question I tried to tackle. But I was frequently distracted.

I am in the Beinecke Library at Yale, paddling in the shallows of a great sea, the thousands of pages of the George MacDonald papers. I linger over Lewis Carroll's letters to the MacDonald children. This for example to his favourite among them, Mary MacDonald: 'Just now the Bishop of Oxford came in to see me. It was a civil thing to do and he meant no harm, poor man, but I was so provoked at his coming that I threw a book at his head, which I am afraid hurt him a good deal.'

Another distraction are the wonderful letters to MacDonald from Rose La Touche's mother. She tells him that her daughter – over whom John Ruskin was to break his heart and lose his mind – is suffering from 'one of her mysterious brain attacks'. The cause of this little girl's intense distress, her mother explains, is that at church the previous Sunday she was denied the bread and wine which the rest of her family were given. I pray for the repose of the soul of Rose La Touche at Solemn Mass at Christchurch, New Haven, a vertiginously high church which, it tells the world, 'invites all baptized children to receive communion'.

Whether or not it was good for Hackney that I took some study leave, I'm sure that it was for everyone's benefit that once or twice I came back there from paradise.

The site of the Garden of Eden is not, as you supposed, a parcel of land at the confluence of the Tigris and Euphrates. It is a tiny island in the Baltic. On it is a village of a hundred peaceful homes surrounded by fertile fields. Nowhere is more than a mile from the sea. The islanders live to an extreme old age before dying young. There are many apple trees, none forbidden. These are wreathed in webs woven by spiders unknown elsewhere to natural history. On a morning in May primal things are done around a pole in the village square. No doors are locked. There is a policeman but he has nothing to do. The island has its own micro-climate, escaping by some meteorological mystery the brutal Baltic weather. There is a church but it is sparsely attended. Religion, a consequence of the Fall, has never flourished here. We spent a few days on this island in August and now, as the days draw in, nostalgic for paradise, we go back there in our minds. After all, what else are summer holidays for but to offer solace – 'the evening with the photograph album' – when winter comes? I am not going to tell you the name of my Baltic Eden. Too many visitors and it would be paradise lost.

142

12

God at the Crossroads

God the Father, or someone looking much like him, is often seen in Hackney. He is a tall figure with flowing locks of white hair and he wears a once-white cassock. He regularly stands at a notorious junction, a confusion of five intersecting roads, where drivers dither or rage, where guns are drawn, drugs pushed, suicide contemplated, and where, surely, once loomed the parish gallows. God's look-alike holds high a placard proclaiming doom. I glimpse odd phrases as I dodge the traffic – 'Great tribulation', 'Satan is at large', 'Peace impossible'. I admire this latter-day Ezekiel who continues to testify to Hackney's impudent and stiff-hearted 'whether they hear or whether they forbear'. And I salute the memory of another such prophet, one well-known to all of us who lived and worked in Trafalgar Square, one who in all weathers paced between the pigeons and the tourists with a bill-board bearing the injunction, 'Reduce lust. Avoid protein. Eat fewer nuts.'

On the whole clergy in the inner-city stick to their jobs. Many stay there all their working lives. I think of Father Fred Preston. He spent forty years in the same parish in Hackney, four decades mostly spent visiting. To celebrate his faithful ministry, his congregation threw a party for him. A few hours before it started this wonderful old soldier, deciding that he could do without all the fuss, simply sat down and died. I think too of a retired priest in our parish who told me with pride, 'I've stayed on the same page in the London *A to Z* all my ministry.' One wonders what keeps such clergy going – or, rather, what stops them going, from looking for a living and a life somewhere more salubrious.

The most compelling reason for staying in the inner-city, despite the sense of camping in the crater of a volcano, is the company you keep. I write as one who for many years lived and worked near Godalming in the Surrey 'white highlands'. To be sure, it is just as hard to love God and serve your neighbour in Godalming as it is in Hackney. I salute the clergy who minister to the good folk of Godalming, to those who take the train to town each day, who make a lot of money in the city, and who have the ulcers and unhappy families to prove it. But I was never tempted to go back there. Once you have lived in technicolour you have no desire to return to monochrome.

I browse in my diary and I recall some of the characters whom I met in Hackney and who enriched my life there. I have especially fond memories of Doreen.

When we lived in Trafalgar Square we used to take our guests to the National Gallery. Now we take them round the corner to Doreen's Pet Parlour. It is a wonderful place, crowded with beasts that only East Enders would have the bottle to buy as pets – foul-mouthed parrots, razor-toothed rodents capable of carnage inside your armchair or trousers, nameless creatures with scales, forked tongues and lidless eyes, gross fish. The shop is rich in ripe pongs and a good game with the kids is to see who can count the most. But something very sad has happened. Someone's nicked the python. She was the prize of the parlour and there is grief and outrage locally that she should have been stolen. (There was a sign on her tank telling you that she was fed on traffic-wardens.) It is hard to see how she can be disposed of. Like a cartoon of Michelangelo, she is too well-known to be sold on the open market. Perhaps she has already been turned into soup or handbags. Or perhaps she has swallowed her thief for starters and is now out there somewhere looking for the next course. Mind where you tread.

Alas, Doreen had to move. Like many another small shop-keeper she fell victim to the might and greed of Tescos. One of my first battles in the borough was on her behalf.

Ahab, son of Omri, is planning to open a Tescos hypermarket in the heart of Hackney. First the neighbourhood Naboths have to be bought out, including Doreen. It will be a tragedy if her shop goes and not only because you will have to go so much further to sex your newts. The loss will be of an establishment, so few remaining in the East End, where the immemorial dignities of sale and purchase are honoured and the exchange between merchant and customer is made with gravity and joy. Doreen's is a shop like all the little shops once were, even if they didn't all sell aardvarks. So much about Doreen's is good and free, the laughter, the advice, the kind words. But Ahab wants her out. Wrapped in Elijah's mantle, I have written to Ahab. I have told him that if he forces Doreen out the Lord will be very angry and that he will make the house of Tesco like the house of Jeroboam, son of Nebat and like the house of Baasha, son of Ahijah. And I have added that if it comes to blood having to be licked up Doreen only has to release her stock on to the pavement.

Tescos of course won. Tescos always does. Her wonderful shop had to relocate. Doreen retired, but her family still runs the business. I dropped by most weeks for cat litter and a chat. There are all sorts of intoxicating plans for a brave new Hackney as with its neighbouring boroughs it hosts the 2012 Olympics. I don't suppose that Doreen and her menagerie feature in those plans. But it will be otherwise in the city to come, of which Hackney, inner-city of God, is the promise. There the lion will lie down with the lamb – and the parrot nest in the coils of the python.

Doreen's new shop is just round the corner from what was our Rectory. Even closer, between our back-gate and the church, was another establishment with a sure source of customers.

Hackney Rectory is next-door-but-one to the local morgue. On the 'beginning at Jerusalem' principle I pay an early visit. The young woman on duty gives me a graphic account of the sad but necessary business of the place, to provide brief lodging for those whose passing was violent or mysterious. I am told about refrigeration and deep-freeze facilities, about what is done with what is left after an autopsy, about the disagreeable aspects of the work in a long hot summer. I hear myself saying, my voice pitched a note too high, 'If we can be of any help do get in touch.' I am reluctant to speculate on the circumstances in which this offer might be taken up. I turn to go, but find that I am unable to shift the bolt on the door. With no trace of a smile the attendant says, 'It's like that to stop anyone getting out.' I notice with alarm that she is wearing a Dracula T-shirt.

Lots of different T-shirts are worn in Hackney. It is a noisy marketplace for political and religious ideas in which competition for custom is fierce. I had only to step outside my door to be in the middle of that market.

There they all are, at the bottom of our drive. The Socialist Workers Party wants me to sign a petition for our troops to be brought home by Christmas. A shady character is selling dodgy CD players. Nearby CND have set up a table. It is nice to know they're still around. Once I was a keen member. As a schoolteacher I declared my Religious Studies department a nuclear-free zone. Then there is this chap in a dog collar. He sits in a chair on the pavement with an empty chair in front of him. Hovering around are his acolytes, young people who are stopping passers-by to ask if they'd like to be prayed for. Before long he has a customer, a woman who sits in the vacant chair in floods of tears. I am curious about this street ministry. Later, when his trade has tailed off, I have a chat with him. He tells me that he is from 'The Universal Church of the Kingdom of God'. A swift Google reveals that this outfit is based in the Rainbow Theatre, Finsbury Park, where its exorcisms and its 'tithe today and get rich tomorrow' preaching have received mixed reviews.

With a whispered 'Jesus loves you' the man outside the McDonalds at the end of our drive presses a tract into my hand. It lists the blessings that will 'literally run me down' if I receive Jesus into my heart and life. 'The crops of your field shall bring forth even in times of famine.' 'Your bank account shall be blessed.' And, more alarmingly, 'The womb of your body shall be blessed.' If I want to find out more I am invited to sit under Pastor Harmony Felix of the 'Mighty Word Ministries' at 2.45 p.m. on Sunday in the St John's Ambulance Hall, Clapton. It is easy to mock. But Pastor Felix is only taking sides, as take sides we all must, in the oldest theological controversy of them all, the quarrel between Deuteronomy ('Obey God, and you'll never have it so good') and Job ('Obey God, and you'll end up on a tip scraping your boils with a broken flower-pot'). Are we promised caviare or Calvary? Across the centuries the debate has swung to and fro. Now it seems that one side is finally winning.

This 'prosperity gospel', the mutant of Christianity which claims that God will reward you materially if you put enough money in the collection to maintain your pastor in the lifestyle to which he has become accustomed, is cornering the market in Hackney. The Kingsway International Christian Centre, about which the Charity Commissioners have had their misgivings, attracts a bigger congregation that any other church in Europe. On any Sunday more worshippers turn up at the KICC evening service than all those going to church that day at all Anglican churches of Hackney put together.

The preacher bounds around a platform as big as a tennis court. 'Are you listening to me tonight?' he shouts. They certainly are – all five thousand of them. They roar 'Amen' as he hammers his message home, each point accompanied by an assenting riffle from the cymbals. 'God will move against nature to bless you – No matter what the doctor says, no matter what the cancer says, you shall be blessed!' His asides are telling. 'I am sure that Saint Paul wrote Hebrews.' 'Don't let them tell you that the world is millions of years old. It was created six thousand years ago.' 'Don't worry about all that ozone stuff.' There is a constant exchange between pulpit and people. 'Somebody say, "He provides!"' The response is a single thunderous echo – 'He provides!' It is exchange without dialogue – putty does not answer back. I stay to the end of the hour-long sermon and then slip out, avoiding the collection. It was my first visit to the Kingsway International Christian Centre which meets in a vast converted warehouse next to what was the Hackney Dog Track. On my arrival at least six stewards shook my hand in welcome. Lots of those huge floppy Bibles were in evidence. (How I coveted one of those in my devout but desiccated Baptist boyhood!) The singing was visceral, not least of the repeated refrain – belted out by the 99% black congregation – 'The blood of Jesus washes white as snow'. I left with a splitting headache.

KICC is on the move. Its present site is required for the 2012 Olympics. The Kingsway Centre will be assisted in its plans to build a vast new mega-church in Rainham by a grant from the London Development Agency – that is to say, the taxpayer – of over £13,000,000. No doubt KICC will interpret that windfall as proof of what they preach.

The proliferation and power of the 'prosperity churches' in Hackney – the great Behemoth of the KICC and the scores of tiny groups in the neighbourhood propagating the same 'gospel' – present a problem to the mainstream churches. Loud emotionally-charged worship, obsession with demons (as I write, memories of the Victoria Climbie case are raw), and claims of miraculous healings make a cocktail which most Anglicans find unpalatable. More precisely, most white British Anglicans find it distasteful, a qualification which highlights why the issue of inter-church relations in the inner-city is so sensitive. The 'prosperity churches' in the East End are all predominantly black churches. So I must ask myself whether my antipathy to them is simply a cultural aversion to attitudes and ways of worship with which I am not familiar. Or are there more objective criteria for what properly constitutes Christian faith and devotion? What is certain is that building a bridge between those who preach that Christian faith boosts your bank balance and those who, with Bonhoeffer, warn that Christ calls us to die has so far proved beyond the engineering skills of Hackney's ecumenical movement.

Ecumenism, if by that we understand the attempt to get the different Christian denominations to unite organizationally, is clearly a lost cause and a waste of time. Should Methodism embrace episcopacy? I suspect that most Hackney Methodists are no more interested in that question than I am. It is impossible to exaggerate the utter irrelevance of such issues to Hackney's murderous sub-culture of drugs and guns or to overstate the giddy futility of discussing them. An infinitely more important issue than ecumenical relationships – in Hackney, as in any inner-city that is home from home to everyone from everywhere – is interfaith relationships. I am ashamed to think how little bridge-building I did in Hackney. I am glad, though, to have had a walk-on part in some worthwhile events.

> Kosher sherry and nibbles last night in the Mayor's Parlour in the Town Hall. It was a reception for four young people from Haifa, two Jews, one Muslim, and one Christian. They are the guests of Hackney, their visit the first of a series of exchanges marking the thirty years that Hackney has been 'twinned' with Haifa. I catch a glimpse of the four teenagers sharing some private joke, perhaps about the ridiculous sight some of us pompous old crumblies are. Clearly they are the best of friends. They are a sign to all of us that we should aim for more than mannered courtesies in our inter-faith relationships. My worry is not that we do not worship together. It is that we so seldom laugh together.

Interfaith dialogue in the inner-city is occasionally conducted by formal consultations. But it went on all the time, I found, once I was out-of-doors.

> A family of Kurdish refugees lives in a couple of rooms above the shop on the corner of our rectory drive. After school their kids kick a football around on the drive and often the ball comes over into our garden. It's the old story. They applied for political asylum four years ago. The parents claim that one of their children was killed by Turkish soldiers. Up to now they have been living in limbo, permission for them to stay being renewed every six months. But now the Home Office has got tough and has decided to deport them. Any day now they will be bundled onto a plane back to a situation which,

rightly or wrongly, they feel is life-threatening. I wrote a letter to the Home Office in support of their appeal for a reprieve. It was the least I could do and I am embarrassed by their gratitude. The children are happily settled in local schools. The family blends perfectly into the box of Bassett's All-Sorts that our neighbourhood already is. But someone, nameless and faceless, says they must go. Another example of 'cruel Britannia'.

I step outside and walk down the street. The dry-cleaners are Turkish, the newsagents are Indian, the carpet store is a Jewish business, the place next-door that will polish your nails – or sell you alarming false ones – is Chinese, the Afro hairdressers ('The Creative Clip-joint') is run by Nigerians, the Halal butchers are Pakistani, next to them is the Vietnamese take-away, the candle shop is Greek . . . The World Parliament of Religions assembles every four years. Between its sessions it meets on my doorstep.

Talking of the Turkish dry-cleaners, this morning I discussed two intractable problems with the manager. The first was an apparently ineradicable stain in the jacket of my best suit, the second was the divinity of Christ. Our dry-cleaner is a Moslem who, like all his co-religionists and unlike most Christians, regards theology as both a natural and an important topic of conversation. I recalled those shining lights and inseparable names, Temple Gairdner and Douglas Thornton, masters of Arabic and saints of God, who a century ago settled in Cairo and whose days were spent in deep unhurried conversation with educated Moslems. There were some converts but countless more drank at the sweet well of their humanity. Thornton burned himself out. (His dying words were 'The work!') Gairdner's prayer that someone would take Thornton's place went unanswered. Writing of 'the reproach of Islam', he said that 'Islam is the greatest call the church has ever had or will have'. That no longer seems such an extravagant claim.

I badly miss my friends and neighbours in Hackney. I particularly miss those I met in church Sunday by Sunday, those to whom I had the impertinence to preach but who taught me far more than ever they learned from me. There were too few pages in my diary for me to pay tribute to all the saints of St John-at-Hackney who touched my life. But some I did mention.

Dr R used to sit at the very back of the church. He didn't always stay for all the service. Quite often he would slip out and take a shower. (The shower is there for clients of our week-day drop-in centre, but it's available on Sundays too. People sometimes feel they need it. It depends who's preaching.) Dr R was a generous man, often pressing little gifts on us. He would share his anxieties too, fears which in time became less and less rational. Few knew that Dr R had once been a leading cardiologist. He had studied medicine in Paris. He had practised in France, in Sweden, and in his native Syria. Nearer home, he had worked in Hackney's old 'Mothers Hospital'. He continued to read the medical journals long after he retired. Dr R was later joined by his brother, Professor S, who in his day had been an eminent civil-engineer. The two brothers looked after each other, retreating into increasingly reclusive lives, fearful of the wicked world beyond their heavily-bolted front door. Dr R died a few weeks ago. At his funeral there was only his brother and one of our congregation to say good-bye to him. Professor S followed the coffin into the cemetery chapel, trundling his computer on a little trolley and clutching several super-market carrier-bags containing his software. After the committal Professor S found it very hard to leave the grave-side. Eventually he gathered all his stuff and we gave him a lift back, not to his lonely flat but to Tescos where he insisted he had to get some yogurt. Dr R touched the lives of thousands. Just the three of us saw him buried. I want to believe that, beyond the river, he has been welcomed home by rather more.

Sim, who lives in a care home, has been worshipping with us for many years. He has severe learning difficulties, but he is a very gentle person and is held in honour and affection by us all. His silence is of one contemplating secrets undisclosed to the noisy and distracted. Last Sunday he disappeared. He was there in church – and then he wasn't. A massive hunt was launched. Police dogs nosed in vain into unsavoury and unvisited recesses of our cavernous church. Two days later Sim was found. Later we pieced together what had happened. Sim had wandered out of church and had got on a bus. Alighting at the terminus, he found himself outside a big building with open doors. He went in and found a seat. There he sat for fourteen hours. At 2.00 a.m. on the Monday a doctor saw Sim. Sim had stumbled into the accident and emergency unit of an East End hospital. The doctor found nothing wrong with him and told him to go. So Sim went and sat down again – for a further twenty-nine hours. At 7.00 a.m. on the Tuesday he was noticed by somebody who said something to somebody else. Three hours later, a social worker began to make some phone calls. At 12 noon Sim's care-workers came to collect him. Fortunately they had brought some food and drink, for it had not occurred to anyone at the hospital to offer this stricken old man even a cup of tea or a glass of water. On his way back, Sim broke his silence. 'This is a nice car ride,' he said.

He came to us as one unknown, the stranger at the back of church. I sensed that here was someone not easily deceived, one who would see through the sophistries to which we default, we who spend too long in pulpits. I was right. John is an actor and actors know when drama turns charade. Half a dozen of us went to see John in a production of T. S. Eliot's *The Cocktail Party* at the Courtyard Theatre, just over the road from Kings Cross. The six of us were a third of the audience in a space seating sixty. But good theatre, like good religion, is more often than not found at the fringe. The opening scene is set at the party of the play's title. Guests chatter inanely. Some distance from them stands a solitary figure, 'the unidentified guest' whose intervention in their empty lives will deliver them from the doom awaiting them, 'the final desolation of solitude in the phantasmal world'. This was John's part. (I tease him that he was type-cast, that his role on stage was the same as in our congregation. He's here to sort us out.)

Apart from Shakespeare's *King Lear*, *The Cocktail Party* has meant more to me than any other play. Its theme is the only question that matters, 'What must I do to be saved?' Eliot's answer is that for some the way of salvation leads to crucifixion 'very near an anthill'.

For others, for most of us, what is required is simply that we 'make the best of a bad job'. 'Both ways are necessary,' Eliot tells us. And, he adds, 'Neither way is better'. Most sermons start from the contrary premise, that striking out for the spiritual summit is always superior to stumbling about in the foothills. So too do most hymns. ('Take my life . . .' and so on.) 'The best of a bad job', we're told, is necessarily a second-best. This primal untruth is at the root of untold anguish, the torment of those who cannot believe that they are good enough. But Eliot understood that we don't all have to be spiritual athletes. Neither way is better. As John himself put it when we met with him later – over cocktails – to discuss the play, 'It's OK to be OK.'

John came to us 'as one unknown'. So too did Laura. The inner-city lets you be inconspicuous. Many who live in the inner-city welcome the anonymity it allows them. In the inner-city you have to recognize that not everyone who enters your church wants you to walk into their life. So it was a little while before we got to know Laura. When we did, we came to appreciate her rare gifts – not least her willingness to become one of our churchwardens.

Laura's voice, like Cordelia's 'ever gentle, soft and low', carries great weight in the counsels of our church. That same voice is well-known to the residents of Marfa, a one-horse town deep in the heart of Texas. Laura has often visited Marfa. When last there she made a live broadcast on the local radio station. She read aloud – it took her six hours to do so – Marfa's telephone directory. The broadcast is now available on two CDs in an attractive presentation pack. To hear Laura reading the phone-book is to experience the numinous. 'ABC Pump and Welding Incorporated, Abuse Hot-line for the Elderly, Jiminez Busstop, Child Obesity Hot-line, Couch Ministries (to which I feel called), Easy-liquor Store, Freedom Bail Bonds, Gonzalez Floorshop . . .' And so on and on until we come finally to the prolific Zubiatis. The music of these names is 'like the slow march of some Gregorian psalm'. The railroad runs by Marfa's radio station. Occasionally Laura must pause as a freight train trundles by, the mournful whistle of its engine sounding a plaintive coda to the solemn roll-call. Here is a strangely beautiful work. What next? I would love to listen to Laura reading Crockfords Clerical Directory. 'Aagaard, Angus Robert; Abayomi-Cole, Bimbisara Alfred; Abbey, Canon Anthony James . . .' So great a cloud of witnesses. On a week's retreat we could hear of them all.

It was a great privilege to be invited back to Hackney to preach at Laura's wedding. Laura and Jonathon met among the ducks in the Serpentine. Jonathon sometimes wears a 'Love me, love my bike' T-shirt. That will be no problem for Laura, who also likes bicycles. The one she rode round Hackney was as high as a horse. When she parked it outside the Rectory I felt I should give it a lump of sugar. One of the readings they chose for their wedding was the conclusion of T. S. Eliot's *The Four Quartets*, 'We shall not cease for exploration . . .' and so on. Had they read the rest of the poem, they might not have asked me to preach. Eliot has been charged with several antipathies. The accusation that he was ageist sticks. 'Do not let me hear of the wisdom of old men,' he writes, 'but rather of their folly.' No doubt he had retired Rectors in mind. The feast, the cabaret, and the dancing that followed the wedding were all in the church. My wife and I graced the floor around the font for a couple of slow numbers. That was something we'd not done while I was still in post.

The jollities resumed the following morning down by the Serpentine. There was no need to break the ice, which members of the Serpentine Swimming Club cheerfully do at chillier seasons. The Club did us proud. Pimms flowed. We sang the club's anthem 'O my darling Serpentine', including the ribald verses. A senior member played some Mozart on his bicycle pump. (The loves of swimming and cycling are twin passions.) A race was raced and to no one's astonishment it was won by Nick, who while still a teenager swam the Channel both ways. The Serpentine Swimming Club is a paradigm of what one day by the grace of God the church of God might become. The affection members have for each other is only matched by the warmth of their welcome to those that join them. There are no hierarchies and – except for those who wear wet-suits – no heretics.

A sadder reason for returning to Hackney, as I noted in my diary, was to preach at the funeral of someone dear to us all at St John's.

Alec, sacristan and verger at St John-at-Hackney for forty years, has died. Alec was brought up in an Irish orphanage. There he froze in winter and was famished all the year round. Alec never complained. When he left the orphanage he went to work on a farm, where he lifted potatoes for a pittance. He never complained. He came to London, where he got a job at the National Gallery. He spent each day sitting in a corner of one or other of the Gallery's rooms making sure no one nicked a Rembrandt. It was tedious work, but he never complained. Often Alec and I would chat about the rectors he had seen come and go and their ridiculous whims and fads. One of my predecessors hated the colour green. If Alec had arrayed the altar in green, he would be told to change the frontal to something more cheerful. Alec did so – and never complained.

During the week Alec would potter around the church doing odd jobs. He always wore his old cloth cap. I never suggested he remove it. If bishops can wear silly hats in church, saints like Alec can surely wear sensible ones. Alec reminded me of Bontche Schweig, of whom the rabbis speak. Bontche endured much in his lifetime, but his response to all his sufferings was to keep silence. After Bontche's death he was brought before the heavenly tribunal that would determine his eternal destiny. The 'defending angel' told the court how through all his many afflictions Bontche had remained silent. Then the 'prosecuting angel' stood to accuse him. He surveyed the court sternly and Bontche Schweig trembled. But then he smiled and when he spoke his words were brief. 'He was silent. I shall be silent too.'

Saints are not all church-goers. Sophie, as far as I know, isn't. But she walks with God – or, to be precise, she cycles with God. Sophie is an artist. She runs the art project 'Vision Impossible', one of the many activities on offer in the centre for Hackney's homeless based in our church. Sophie believes that there is a creative spark in all of us. Thanks to Sophie, there are now established artists in London who once were on the streets. It was Sophie who helped them discover their gifts and who taught them the skills that enabled them to turn their lives around. But Vision Impossible costs money. So, accompanied by Almighty God, Sophie got on her bike. I wrote about her ride in my diary.

> Sophie's back. Sophie took four and a half months to cycle four and a half thousand miles round New Zealand. She did this to raise money for 'Vision Impossible'. Sophie had thirteen punctures (nine in one day), a blow-out tyre, several broken spokes, and a 'rounded chain set', whatever that is. She cycled an average of sixty-five miles a day on a machine which, loaded with all she needed for the journey, weighed 50 kg. She was constantly attacked by sand-flies and mosquitoes. Crossing a mountain pass, she was blown off her bike into a vicious thorn bush. She had to heave her bike over fallen trees and to pedal through floods. She met a lot of taciturn sheep and some astonishingly kind people. At a recent service Sophie told us about her adventures. 'I must admit this trip restored my faith in people,' she said. 'I never felt alone. I did talk to God a lot. I know he must have thought me crazy, but he never tired of my solitary chit-chat and pleas for help.' Sophie did all this because she believes that the homeless do not live by bread alone. Retrospective sponsoring is invited.

The communion of saints is an extended family. The company of those I count as the saints of St John-at-Hackney includes some who took us to their hearts, although they were never able to come and see us. I paid tribute in my diary to one dear to us at St John's, but whose praise is in all the churches.

> A week or two before Christmas a friend phoned to tell us that Nadir Dinshaw had died. Our grief at this news was compounded by receiving two days later a Christmas card from him. Some years ago Nadir had got to hear about our work among Hackney's homeless and so,

every quarter, there came a donation to our church. But such was the exquisite generosity of this extraordinary man that he took us to his heart as a family and often, as with this Christmas card, there was a personal gift for us too. We never met our benefactor but we came across many others who had been blessed by his friendship and benevolence. Nadir's giving was a mighty river the measure of which is only now beginning to emerge. He came from a wealthy Zoroastrian family but later he became an Anglican. Yet neither his Anglicanism nor indeed his Christianity was partisan. His profound spirituality transcended all our confessional constructs, a liberality of heart and mind he had learned from the towering figure of Charlie Andrews. I shall treasure Nadir's card with his last words to us. 'I do so hope all is well with you and yours.' (The 'so' is underlined twice.) And he adds, 'Isn't Rowan's appointment marvellous?'

Nadir, like Alec our verger, like most of Hackney's saints, has joined 'the church expectant', those whose day among us is done and who await a brighter dawn. Unless he has survived into extreme old age, so too has Arthur.

Arthur Atkinson was a Boy Scout and a Salvation Army bandsman. On and off throughout 1916 he kept a diary. That diary turned up the other day – among the *Readers Digest* condensed novels, the Mills and Boon romances, the back numbers of *The People's Friend* – at a book sale at the Clapton Salvation Army citadel. It cost me 75p. The 1916 Scout Diary allowed only a small space for each day and young Arthur's entries are necessarily laconic. For his birthday on 9 January he was given a tenor horn. Now he can play in 'the big band'. Two days later he notes that he 'helped to bring a lad round who had a fit'. In the spring he starts work at 'the Mill'. He's put to work on the 'the cutting machine' and his wages are twelve shillings a week. He never misses band practice or the Sunday services. At an evangelistic rally on 18 June three come forward to the penitent form. Next Thursday he takes his working boots to the cobblers. The only hint of a world at war is the entry for 9 August. 'Saw a searchlight for the first time.' It's a hot summer and he swims a lot. One proud entry reads, 'Swam nearly a breadth under water'. His record of Friday 22 September is fuller than most, 'Brought 16s 8d home. Had my hair cut and had some stuff put on my wart. Went to the library.' A week later he is having a corn removed. There was a special meeting on 9 October. 'Adjutant Peck gave a lecture on India. Very good. He showed us Idols, etc.'

Beyond what these terse jottings tell me, Arthur Atkinson, I know nothing of you and yet my heart reaches out to you. I hope that you went on to have a happy life. And when the roll is called up yonder – if I'm there – I'll listen out for your name.

13

In Praise of Cheese

If I had any say in such matters, I would add this prayer to the Order
for the Renewal of Ordination Vows – 'O Lord, Thou who hast called
me to the sacred ministry of Thy Church, make me more like
Ethelstan Cheese.' Cheese spent the first half of the twentieth century
wandering around the Horn of Africa as the spirit moved him. He
was an Anglican priest and a missionary, although no bishop or
missionary society could ever keep track of him. He was neither
catholic, evangelical, nor liberal. He was simply Cheese. His story has
been beautifully told by Philip Cousins in his little book *Ethelstan
Cheese: Saint of no Fixed Abode.* Cheese has long been a comfort. I
reread his life to boost my morale for the annual church meetings and
all the byzantine paperwork which goes with them. Cheese won few
converts, but across the vast and desolate quarter of Africa that he
made his own he was revered as a holy man. His testimony was that
of Abraham who went out 'not knowing whither he went'. Cheese's
witness was – as it remains – the indictment of the institutional by the
nomadic.

Ethelstan Cheese does not have a holy day all his own. His wonderful name is not in any calendar of greater or lesser festivals. But he
belongs to the 'great cloud of witnesses' who keep us company on
our pilgrimage to the City of God. There is a paradox here. These
'witnesses' of whom the Bible speaks are those who have gone
ahead of us, those whose journey to the Holy City is done. And yet,
it seems, they are still with us, urging us on. It is as if they have
dropped back to steady us when we stumble, to help us up when we
fall, to put us back on the right road when we take a wrong turning.

That is what the saints do for us, both those who have gone
before us and those who are still around. Perhaps it is because I was

159

born on All Saints Day that I have always relied so much on them. I depend on the saints who are in my own family and they have their chapter in this book. I am indebted more than I can say to the saints who are my friends. But equally I owe my spiritual survival to the saints who are now at home with God, but who – it is all so very mysterious – I feel are here at my side.

Many from this 'cloud of witnesses' have come alongside me through what they have written or through what has been written about them. When I left Hackney I had to cull my books, a wretchedly painful exercise. But there were some books I could no more banish than I could slam the door on an old friend. I glance along the shelves that house the remnant of what was once a library and I look at their names, those to whom I have turned – never in vain – when lights were burning low. Charlie Andrews, at whose grave in Calcutta I knelt long ago; Temple Gairdner, who commended Christ so graciously to the Moslem world; his Cairo companion Douglas Thornton, a flame that burned so brightly and so briefly; Thomas Merton, for whom there was nothing left to do after his enlightenment before the great Buddhas of Polunaruwa but to die in a Bangkok bathroom; Simone Weil, who has taught us that nothing is asked of us save our attention and our consent; the Sadhu Sadhu Singh whom little children mistook for Jesus . . . Time would fail to tell of them all.

Often I tried to distil in my diary something of what they have meant to me, these saints who have spoken to me from a book in my hands. Some we have already met – George MacDonald, who was not impressed by Hackney's grandiose parish church; Bernard Walke, who helped me to catch the last of its light before night falls on Cornwall too; Søren Kierkegaard, who did not confuse Christianity with Christendom. But there were many others – all 'strangers and pilgrims on the earth' – who enabled me to run with just a little more patience 'the race set before me', that long haul of my life's wayward ministry whose last lap was through the hectic streets of Hackney.

Not all of the saints who befriended me were conventionally pious. Indeed many of them, like Cheese himself, were not conventionally anything. I think of Archbishop William Ullathorne and Bishop Walter Carey.

Are our modern bishops and archbishops a boring lot? Certainly they are if compared with Archbishop William Ullathorne, who was a missionary in Australia before becoming the first Roman Catholic Bishop of Birmingham. I have been much entertained by his recently republished autobiography *From Cabin-boy to Archbishop*. For a long time the bishop kept a baked human head in a bandbox over his bed. He intended to give it to the monks at Downside, but the maggots got to it first and he was obliged to bury it. Not everyone knows that.

Something of a wimp myself, I have always been an admirer of 'muscular Christianity'. Alas, there are no wholly unreconstructed muscular Christians left, but I now know who was the last of the line. I refer to Bishop Walter Carey, a copy of whose autobiography *Good-bye to my Generation* I picked up second-hand the other day. Walter Carey, uncle of the Carey who mass-produced 'Westcott Man', was a hero of the Battle of Jutland, Warden of Lincoln Theological College, and Bishop of Bloemfontein. Here are some of the Bishop's robust opinions which I have transcribed into my commonplace book.

> On school games: 'Are games overdone? Yes, if you are a long-haired pseudo-intellectualist who thinks that boys are better occupied with James Joyce or Picasso or Stravinsky than with football or cricket or rowing. I don't agree with that crowd.'

> On the twentieth century: 'I reckon that if Hitler had been a rowing Blue or a rugger Blue history would have been different'.

> And on training men for the ministry: 'I made them all join the golf club – so useful in later life'.

Few of today's bishops are as odd. The truth is that that they are not odd enough to be entirely trusted. Much to their disadvantage, they are not to be compared with the Right Reverend Lord Rupert Ernest William Gascoyne Cecil, sixty-fifth Bishop of Exeter, to whom I was introduced by Trevor Beeson.[6] Bishop Gasgoyne had a face like a fish. He rode around on an orange bicycle, except when he absent-mindedly mounted someone else's machine of a different colour. Longer journeys were by train. He depended on his ticket to tell him where he was going, though on arriving anywhere he still would sometimes have to phone his wife, Lady Florence ('Fluffy') Bootle-Wilbraham, to find out where he was. 'Love in a mist', they called him.

We shall not look on their like again. Bishops today must conform to the culture over which they preside, a culture intolerant of the idiosyncratic. Alas, in many a modern diocese it is a case of the bland leading the bland.

Some books are precious to me because they recall scenes from my own story. One book returns me to my schooldays. A slim volume of poems takes me back to a quarter of Cambridge unvisited by tourists. Reading another book, I am once more in a tiny church in Chile.

Peter Baelz, who died recently, was a wonderful man. He played squash for Dulwich. The team's photograph hung in the school tuck shop and, as I champed on a cheese roll one lunch-time, I remember noticing the unusual name and matching it to the ascetic figure in the picture. Baelz's 1974 Bampton Lectures *The Forgotten Dream* struck me at the time as one of the most beautiful and persuasive expositions of the Christian faith I had ever read. Impulsively I wrote to tell him so. His kind reply was revealing. 'As you may have guessed,' he wrote, 'my heart as well as my mind went into *The Forgotten Dream*. Commercially, it was a complete failure . . .' But then Jesus too was remaindered and pulped.

Derek Skeet is dead. The card that tells me of his passing has a picture of harebells and mayweed. Derek was fond of wild flowers and his remote retirement home, beneath great Norfolk skies, was lost in them. In the sixties and seventies he had been head teacher of a primary school in a rough area of Cambridge. The kids no one else could manage all seemed to end up in Derek's school. Derek delighted in his delinquent, nit-ridden, whiffy charges. Our Ridley Hall students were sent to him to find out how to take RE lessons and assemblies. Derek talked to them instead about what it means to be a child. They did not always understand him, for he too spoke in parables. But they saw his genius. Derek loved children. He also loved Cambridge, particularly the dank and neglected vicinity of Jesus Green Lock. There he would walk his dog and compose his poetry:

O cleave a little earth, a little time,
A handful of our separating years
The iron bedrock and the unslaked dust
The fossil buried in the rust of tears
And weep a little when the shoot appears
A little while
A fragment of our love.

Philip Crowe has kindly sent me a copy of his latest book, *Strange Design*. It is a great read, despite its mentioning an event in my past I would prefer to forget. Here I am today, a contented old fuddy-duddy of a liberal, peacefully committed to the view that God lets you get on with things without interfering, and along comes Crowe, publicly reminding me that I once witnessed a miracle. I wrote about it in the now sadly defunct *Crusade* magazine, but that was a quarter of a century ago and I had hoped that by now the dust would have settled. It was in a remote village in southern Chile and the last night of a week-long evangelistic mission. Lots were 'gloriously converted', as we used to say. And they all stayed on to be healed. The evangelist told them, 'Put your hand where you need healing'. Then I saw how the poor suffer, for most there touched their teeth. (No one appeared to have piles.) The evangelist prayed for them – rather loudly I recall – then invited some of them on to the platform, telling them to look into each other's mouths.

Seeing doubting Thomas in the midst, the evangelist hauled me up with them, handed me a torch, and invited me to make my own inspection. Then I saw the cause of the ecstasy around me. Those teeth had been filled, each filling in the shape of a silver cross. Except for one small boy – God keeps his best gifts for children – who showed me a back tooth in which was distinctly set a golden cross. There were no dentists in that part of Chile. Moreover these people were malnourished – they needed food, not fillings, for God's sake! Also a nasty little dictator called Pinochet had just taken over. And I'd seen the gold torn from teeth at Auschwitz – no signs and wonders there. Miracles are appallingly equivocal things. No wonder Jesus told those he healed to keep quiet about it. Perhaps I should have shut up too.

A precious gift is a good book from an old friend. I bathe in the benediction of two such books, both of which confirm that saints break the mould.

William Young, formerly archivist of St Martin-in-the-Fields, has sent me a copy of the history he has edited of Holy Cross Church, Cromer Street, the church where the intimidating and wildly eccentric figure of Father Napier Pitt Sturt ('reminiscent of Queen Mary in widow's weeds') made sure things were done properly. Charles Bonsall has given me a copy of *Running for Revival,* his sister's biography of their father, Henry Brash Bonsall. (There is a PhD to be written about why those zealous for the truth so often have such rococo names.) Brash Bonsall was for many years Principal of the Birmingham Bible Institute. He was a doughty warrior for God, a foe of liberalism in all its hues, and given to praying aloud for you when you weren't expecting it.

A commitment that kept me reading in Hackney was membership of our local clergy reading group. There were rarely more than three or four of us at any one meeting. Was that because clergy are less literate than they used to be? One fears so. (Certainly they are more numerate. They have to be to compile the 'Statistics for

Mission' they have to send to the centre each year.) But perhaps clergy are reluctant to read simply because so many theological books are unreadable. Contemporary theological debate has largely become a conversation between academics talking to each other in a language no one else can understand. 'Radical Orthodoxy', for example, is an influential theological movement. It probably has important things to say to the church. But we shall never know, because the 'radically orthodox' are so wilfully obscure that we have only the most tenuous notion of what they are on about. In our reading group we went for more accessible titles.

> While tucking into our *Mi Tom Cua Xa Xiu, Banh Canh Ga Ca,* and *Hoanh Thanh Bat Buu* we discuss Joseph Perez's new book, *The Spanish Inquisition – A History.* We are meeting and eating in what was once a local public bath-house. (The separate 'his and hers' entrances remain.) Such facilities are no longer needed in the fragrant parish of St Peter, De Beauvoir, and the premises today accommodate a Vietnamese restaurant. We are the Stepney Episcopal Area Reading group and we assemble once a quarter to discuss a book we have studied since the last meeting. The book is disquieting. Our church too wants to make sure its ministers stay 'on message'. The call for 'heresy trials' is once more heard. I do hope that those fearful for my orthodoxy do not press for the methods sanctioned by Torquemeda to secure it. ('Show him the instruments, Mr. Archdeacon.') 'The ordeal by water' sounds particularly disagreeable. But the really dreadful thing about the Torquemeda's Inquisition was not that it was an office of the Church – though it was that – but that it was also a government department. Ideological state dictatorship was the invention neither of Communist Russia nor of Nazi Germany but of Christian Spain.

As my time at Hackney was coming to an end, the debate about whether the Church of England should consecrate women bishops was becoming more heated and acrimonious. There was no doubt at St John-at-Hackney where we stood on this issue. We were blessed by the ministry of a 'non-stipendiary' woman priest whose wisdom and kindness, whose preaching and pastoral skills, were an immeasurable gift to all of us. I realize as I glance along my shelves just how many of the saints who have taken me by the hand and led me on – not without first rapping my knuckles – have been women. I am sickened by the thought of how we men have treated some of them – Mary Ward and Edel Quinn, for example.

Too many books are written in a hurry. By contrast Sister Mary Littlehales's *Mary Ward* was over a quarter of a century in the making. A great biography – and this is one – is born of the companionship of author and subject, a relationship which, like any other, becomes deep and intimate only with the passing of the years. Mary Ward believed that nuns need not necessarily be confined to convents. She also thought that girls should be educated. She wanted the Pope to share her vision and she set out to see him. Sister Mary includes a map of Mary Ward's travels. A broken line zig-zags back and forth across it, tracing the path of her journeys, almost all on foot, across the length and breadth of Europe. Thirty miles a day on roads that, since the sack of Rome, had ceased to be roads. Twice this indomitable woman, famished by hunger and racked by pain, crossed the Alps in winter for the love of God. She and her companions are branded as 'Jesuitesses'. She herself is imprisoned by the Inquisition and condemned by the Church as a heretic and a rebel. Through all these ordeals her serenity of spirit remains as unwavering as her fidelity to her vision.

Mary Ward's importance cannot be exaggerated. In her concern for the education of girls, including the poorest of them, she was far ahead of her time. Her life testifies not only to the cost of discipleship but also to the cost of change. Mountain passes may still have to be crossed in winter. Opponents of Mary Ward made many different malicious and mendacious claims about her, but all traceable to a single incontestable and damning indictment. 'When all is done,' observed the Jesuit Minister, 'they are but women.' Such things may no longer be said but, in institutions with glass ceilings, it would be naïve to suppose that they are not thought.

Energy is released as matter is destroyed. It is the first law both of the universe and of the spirit. The Venerable Edel Quinn (1907–44) spent the second half of her short life dying. She carried in her wasting body the death of Jesus so that the life of Jesus was manifested. Somewhere in the Vatican there are old men sitting round a table, endlessly deliberating whether she should be canonized. It is possible that they are less adept at the charleston than she was. She was as slight and fleet as a sylph, this holy wraith. Thank God, she has now found a biographer with the delicacy and deftness to do her some justice. Much is recorded in Desmond Forristal's *Edel Quinn* that once we were not supposed to know – how her father's compulsive gambling was nearly the ruin of his family, how she delighted in nice clothes, how extraordinarily attractive men found her and the degree of her sacrifice in choosing celibacy. A light is turned on in the life of Dublin's poor to whom her evenings – and often half her nights – were given before she sailed for Africa. Her story reveals what it meant to have tuberculosis before the drugs that would conquer it were discovered. Edel Quinn went to Africa as an envoy of the Legion of Mary. For eight years her bright flame blazed until the little that was left of her was consumed. Those of us who know the ordeal by mud or dust of travel in East Africa can only marvel at the itineraries this frail, lovely, indomitable woman undertook. Her memorial are the scores of branches of the Legion which she founded and, when her name is spoken, the joy in the old eyes of those blessed by her smile more than sixty years ago.

Mary Ward and Edel Quinn were women of fervent faith. Their witness humbles and inspires me. But for my part, I do not find God as evident a reality as they do. That is why I take heart too from those for whom much is uncertain, save the preciousness of our few fleeting days and our duty to love one another, and yet who testify that we may live purposefully and even joyfully.

I have not read all Don Cupitt's books. His rate of publication, like the late Barbara Cartland's, far exceeds my speed of reading. But he says of his latest book, *Philosophy's Own Religion*, that it presents a summary of his own 'final outlook'. Will this really be Don Cupitt's last word to us? We shall see. Be that as it may, I was deeply moved by it. There is a limpid lucidity here, that of a mind which has wrestled until the breaking of the day with deep questions and to which at last all has become clear. But there is too a note of melancholy. Cupitt knows that few are listening. There is little danger that a church now marketing its message in blister-packs will take him seriously. I hope that I will be a better priest because of this book. Cupitt contemplates with equanimity – even with joy – the transience and contingency of things. The absurd structures we are expected to maintain, as do our mortal bodies, all have the sentence of death written across them. Everything comes and everything goes. As someone said – I think I did – 'there will not always be purificators and Deanery Synods'.

When the writer to the Hebrews refers to that 'great cloud of witnesses' surrounding us and urging us on he did not, one presumes, have Bloomsbury in mind. But I am still grateful to Virginia Woolf, if only because in a roundabout way she contributed to the cost of keeping us going in Hackney.

Paramount Films are making a big feature film about Virginia Woolf and today they shoot a sequence in our churchyard. The burned-out bangers around the church have been carted off and replaced by beautiful old Bentleys. Extras in twenties costume promenade our paths. My priestly role in the production has been to touch them for a hefty 'facility fee'. But I would have let them go ahead for nothing. I exchange a few pleasantries with the crew and drift back to my study. I turn to *To the Lighthouse*, Virginia Woolf's most consummate achievement, a text so luminous and profound that there is something of the fourth gospel about it. A little boy longs to sail to a lighthouse and a lonely woman struggles to finish a painting. At the end of the novel the boy, now a young man, at last reaches the lighthouse. And with a final bold stroke of her brush, poor Lily Briscoe completes her picture. Like her own small life, it will soon be forgotten. Yet something has been accomplished. 'It is finished,' says Lily.

It is finished. Some kind of closure is possible. Like George Eliot, whom she both revered and resembled – the epithet 'equine' recurs in recollections of both women – Virginia Woolf lost all faith in purportedly revealed religion. But she possessed instead, rarest of blessings, the gift of sight. 'We must lay upon her grave whatever we have it in our power to bestow of laurel and of rose.'

George MacDonald said that a multitude of misplaced worships will be banished by one good book. He would have enjoyed a writer who has been a tonic to many of us in recent years.

The joy of a holiday is the leisure to read. An undiluted pleasure this year has been Alexander McCall Smith's tales of Precious Ramotswe, Botswana's only female private detective (*The No 1 Ladies' Detective Agency* and sequels). The stories are a delight, blessed by a gentle wisdom and suffused with a deep love of Africa, the continent which, for all its sorrows, bequeaths to all who have once lived there, but who now languish under grey northern skies, a sense of exile never to be assuaged.

I note from one of the stories this passing comment about the problem with governments. 'They want to do things all the time; they are always very busy thinking of what things they can do next. That is not what people want. People want to be left alone to look after the cattle.' I toyed with the idea of running off lots of copies of these words and posting them, each with a compliments slip, to my betters. But my nerve failed. I am probably in enough trouble already.

14

The Inner-City of God

I wander across to the church for one last time. I kick back over the
fence the football which has sailed into our garden from the 'education centre' next door. This is a sin-bin for children who have been
banned from school for bad behaviour. It's more Center Parc than
boot-camp. Next-door to them is the Hackney morgue. Outside is a
white van. 'Dimmock's Refrigeration Services', it says on the side.
The weather is still quite mild, so let's hope they do a good job. I stroll
through the churchyard. After decades of neglect by the council, this
fine garden in the heart of Hackney is being restored. I notice that a
mountain of steaming manure as big as a bus has been deposited
opposite the church porch. There is something richly redolent about
this pile of muck before our doors. At St John-at-Hackney we have
been 'going for growth'. Standing down-wind, I savour this 'fresh
expression of church'. The work in the churchyard has included the
refurbishment of some of our handsome tombs. I'm pleased to see
that they have done up the splendid Loddiges tomb. The Loddiges
were great horticulturalists. Conrad Loddiges introduced rhubarb
into Britain. Have I done anything half as useful, I wonder, in my
time in Hackney?

I was aware that clergy do not always retire gracefully. Some have a
pathological need to be needed. They dread the time when they will
be no longer wanted. Some like the sound of their own voice – one
dear to me says that I do – and they grieve that it will fall silent.
Some delight in a role which permits them to appear in public in
funny clothes. Many feel that at long last they are just beginning to
learn what it is all about and they are sad that it is now too late to
tell people what they have discovered. Many worry about how they
will manage on a miniscule pension. There are those who dread

what they have frequently pronounced about from their pulpits – the condition and consequence of our mortality. Given that we all have so much to worry about, I was therefore surprised to find myself mixing with a singularly merry lot on the pre-retirement course I attended. It was organized by the Southwark diocese and took place at the cathedral.

> The sessions were energetically chaired by a canon of the cathedral decades younger than the rest of us. She began by telling us that the facilities were downstairs and along several corridors. For those already deep in bus-pass territory this was bad news. We learned that some clergy retirement homes are more sought-after than others. It is much like entering your boy for Eton – you need to get your name down fast. A nice doctor told us what to do to keep in good nick as age kicks in. We must not be ashamed of sleeping after lunch. Diet and weight must be reduced. Watch out for hospitals. These may cure you, but they won't care for you. Don't hit the bottle just before bedtime. Bishop Colin Buchanan talked about 'the theology of retirement'. The mantra 'You are ordained for life' was intoned. I find this obvious truth far from obvious. When I retire to Brighton I intend to take a part-time job. If people ask me what I do, I shall tell them that I used to be a priest but now I am a deck-chair attendant. That seems to me perfectly reasonable and that is what I wanted to say. But I didn't dare.

A number of other Hackney incumbents were in terminal negotiations with the Church of England Pensions Board about the time I was. We – 'the old dogs' – were asked to conduct our triennial three-day chapter conference. We met at St Columba's, Woking. They have revamped the place since I was last there. They have a sophisticated new toaster which has to be mastered if you want breakfast. Beside it is a placard with operating instructions as complicated as the preface to the *Common Worship Lectionary*. Hackney's younger clergy, of course, take the new technology in their stride, just as they know what 'ordinary time' is. Thanks to them I got some toast.

Another conference was going on while we were there, a meeting of the Lambeth Palace staff. There were distant glimpses of Archbishop Rowan Williams, looking surprisingly chirpy. These exalted beings met in the house. We, lesser fry, were dispatched to the conservatory. There is a lot of glass in the new St Columba's. Unfortunately, they built this conservatory under an old oak tree and our deliberations were punctuated by the noise of acorns dropping on the glass above us. As an old soldier, I found the sound familiar. The detonations sounded exactly like the sharp crack of rifle fire. I swiftly suppressed the thought that what we were hearing was the sound of the Lambeth staff being taken out one by one and shot. But the archbishop did look so very cheerful.

I introduced the session I was down for by sketching my own theological journey. I spoke of the experience in my life closest to what once happened on a Damascus road. For Paul, the light blazed. For me, thirty years ago in a seedy transport café in Derbyshire, the light guttered out. (I was on my way to Swanwick to give a 'keynote' at a conference.) All at once, over a mug of tepid tea and a slab of tired cake, the Christian story, with all its unlikely claims, collapsed like a house of cards. I told the chapter that my journey since then had been a search for sight. Occasionally there have been glimpses of 'men as trees walking'. I shared with the brethren how my companion on that search has been someone on a much more important quest than mine.

I first read Schweitzer's *Quest of the Historical Jesus*[7] – or tried to – when I thirteen. Yes, I was a sad little boy. Schweitzer's *Quest* is still the book I would take with me to my desert island. Schweitzer himself has long been dethroned. His interpretation of the mission of Jesus is derided. We are told that the hospital he ran for half a century in equatorial Africa was both unhygienic and racist. For all I know, they now write off Schweitzer's book on Bach and say that he was a rubbish organist. But one thing Schweitzer did understand. He recognized that Jesus remains an enigma and that all our attempts to demystify him, from Chalcedon to Alpha, are unavailing. As I shred a lifetime's sermons, I realize that I know little more about that strange peripatetic Galilean exorcist than did the lonely child I once was. He comes to me, now as then, as one unknown.

A good question was put to me more than once while I was in Hackney. 'What keeps you going?' The question is a razor. It cuts through all the pulpit pieties. Answer it, if you dare, and you bare your soul. It is easy enough to list sources which do not sustain the spirit – *Alpha News*, catalogues published by clerical outfitters, Leviticus, radical orthodoxy, deanery synods, the canons of the Church of England, altar linen, 'worship songs', the Athanasian Creed, and so on and on. These are ashes, not bread. So what – and who – kept me going in my incomparable and impossible parish? First, the love and forgiveness of family and friends. Secondly, all the spiritual mavericks and misfits, Cheese and the rest, 'strangers and pilgrims' all of them, who lent their quirky companionship on the lonely road. Thirdly, George MacDonald who beheld our church building and wept over it. Fourthly, Lear, redeemed in the wilderness. Then, of course, there was Jesus of Nazareth, and the haunting tales of him the Gospels tell. And, above all, the saints of St John-at-Hackney, the punters who – 'behold, I show you a mystery' – bucked the trend by pitching up at church in increasing numbers. These were unfailing springs.

During my last few days as rector I was more worried about what I should say in my last sermon than what I would do when the preaching had to stop. As I noted in my diary, a peer of the realm came to my rescue.

Monday 1 March 1880 was a good day for Lord Algernon George Lawley, fifth Baron Wenlock. He was in India as the guest of the Maharajah of Cooch Behar. He writes in his diary, 'After tiffin had a tremendous hooroosh after a rhino'. Algy Lawley's family owned half of Yorkshire. He went to Eton and Cambridge where, as a peer of the realm, he could take a degree without sitting an exam. His student days were spent hunting and socialising with the fast set. But something else was obviously going on, because he ended up here in the

East End as one of my predecessors. He lived a life of the utmost austerity, we are told. He never went to any meetings. ('Who is going to do the visiting?' he asked.) He was much loved. He was rector here at St John-at-Hackney from 1897–1911. A day or two before I retired a friend passed on to me a fascinating memoir of him ('printed for private circulation'). This rare little book contains the text of his last sermon at St John's and I quoted from it in my own valedictory homily. Algy Lawley spoke of what he owed to the saints of St John-at-Hackney. They were for him, he said, 'a ladder of life, set up here on earth, in the most unlikely of spots, bringing us near to the Vision of God, in a land very far off, and yet near'. Amen to that.

The end of our journey, the healing of our sorrows, the silencing – if not the answering – of our questions, will be 'the Vision of God'. So said the Reverend Lord Algernon Lawley and so say all the saints. Of that vision we cannot speak directly. We can only use picture-language. Algie Lawley speaks of 'a land very far off, and yet near'. The image he uses is of the Christian's 'promised land', where we shall reign and rest when our wilderness wanderings are done.

Another scriptural image of the vision that will bless our waking eyes is that of the City of God. The image of the city represents both everything we must abjure and all we must seek. Our Christian journey starts with the gates of a city shutting behind us. Jesus died 'outside the city gate' and, if we would save our souls alive, we must flee the city to join him (Hebrews 13.12). We have nowhere else to go. 'Here we have no lasting city, but we are looking for the city which is to come' (Hebrews 13.14). The city we must flee represents the old order. It stands for what we know as 'religion', for what has been well called 'the petrifaction' of the way of Jesus. Jesus founded his church on a rock. We have fossilized it in structures. Religion makes relating to God a matter of complying with the procedures by which the powerful seek to control our access to him. The Church of England is a religious organization. It puts up barriers. We have seen, for example, how it still stops children from sharing communion with the rest of the family. Jesus broke all such barriers. As a consequence he was crucified 'outside the city' and, if we want to join him, that is where we must regroup.

Does 'fleeing the city' mean leaving the church? Many in our own day, ordained and lay, have done so and have found their departure liberating. They have discovered spiritual enrichment and the kindly fellowship of kindred spirits in places where the debates of General Synod are wasted breath and the deliverances of the Archbishops' Council are wasted paper. They have found themselves nearer Jesus and more certain of his way now that they are no longer required to stand for the next hymn, to pay for repairs to the roof, to say together the words in bold print, or to defend the apparent misogyny and homophobia of many of their co-religionists.

Others – I am one – have chosen to stay. That choice is, no doubt, perverse and illogical, given the distance between the Jesus we meet in the gospels and the structures in which we try to contain him. But even if 'staying on and staying in' is hard to justify, perhaps there are considerations in whose light we can be forgiven for doing so. The Spirit, blowing where he wills, cannot be confined to institutional channels, but by the same token he cannot be kept out of them. Bones can live, including those of the Church of England. We know that from the experience of that crazed seer Ezekiel and from what happened on the first Easter Day. I know it to be so from my time as Rector of Hackney, where – even in 'the ugliest building in Christendom, bar one' – the breath of God breathed on us and gave us new life. It seems, paradoxically, that we can 'flee the city', as we must, but still turn up at church occasionally.

Our journey begins with the gates closing behind us. Our journey ends with gates opening to us when, our long exile over, we are at last welcomed home. We are on our way to the City of God. Although Hackney falls far short of heaven, for me there was much about Hackney that made the rumours of that other city ring true. That is why I shall always think of it as 'the inner-city of God'.

I think of Hackney's children. For all the problems of our huge church building, children always found it fun to explore, and its vast spaces gave them plenty of room to run around. Now that it is at last restored, our churchyard too is somewhere where children may safely play. I think again of that text that was once on my wall, the promise that the streets of the city we are heading for 'shall be full of boys and girls playing' (Zechariah 8.5).

I think of Hackney's poorest, of the many in the borough, as in every inner-city neighbourhood, who are homeless or whose 'homes' are a travesty of all that that lovely word suggests. In our day-centre we tried to provide for them 'a place of refuge and a place of change'. That is how we put it. And that too is how the New Testament speaks of what we are promised in the City of God. We shall rest – and we shall be made new.

I think of Hackney's 'community of communities'. We longed that our church should not be a ghetto, but a fellowship open and attentive to the insights of all who seek for truth and who bear witness to that truth from the vantage points of their own traditions. As well as sharing our own 'good-news', we sought the common-ground on which we could work together to serve our neighbourhood. It is said of the city of God that 'the kings of the earth will bring their glory into it' (Revelation 21.24). They will bring *their* glory into the city. '*Our* glory', as it were, is to have recognized God in the face of Jesus. But as we throng before the gates of the Holy City, where the myriad paths towards it meet, we shall rejoice with those who have seen the glory of God in other faces and who have known him under other names. Lots of those crowding there will be from Hackney.

And I think too, as I leave Hackney, of John the Baptist. Our church was dedicated to him. There he was, in the stained-glass window I looked at across the congregation when I stood at the altar. There he was, tucking into his locusts one by crunchy one, each garnished with a smearing of honey. There he was, his camel-skins no more comic a costume than my cassock-alb.

I found John the Baptist a constant inspiration. He taught me my job in Hackney. He also made clear to me what is the residual role of the Christian church now that, at last, it must forfeit its social standing and surrender its privileges. John the Baptist had a lot to say, not least about the abuse of power and the paramount claims of the poor. But the heart of his message can be distilled in just one of his words – 'Look'. 'Behold the Lamb of God.' John pointed to Jesus. And then he got out of the way.

My task too was to try to let Jesus be seen. I had to do my best not to misrepresent him or to mislead people about him. Like John, I had to say, 'Look!' I had to do what I could to allow Jesus to be seen – in all his mystery – and then I had to stand aside, allowing people to make of this enigmatic but compelling figure whatever they would.

That too is the church's job, in the inner-city as everywhere else. Our task is John the Baptist's, the last and greatest of the prophets, who was content to gesture towards his Lord and then to slip away. 'He must increase, I must decrease,' said John (John 3.30). We point to Jesus – and then we clear off so that we do not block the sight-lines of any who care to look his way. That is the church's residual role. All along it has been the church's only *distinct* role. Everything else the church has done – in its schools, in its social and development work, in its hospitals, and the rest – has been a mission to be shared with all people of goodwill and not its own unique task.

We point to Jesus, but we do not presume to dictate what people's response to him should be. As in Galilee, so in Hackney. People must make of Jesus whatever they choose. After all, who on earth are we to say who he really is?

We point to Jesus. So why don't people see him? Often it is because the church gets in the way, because it scatters the path to Jesus with all manner of 'stumbling-blocks', obstacles for people to fall over as they try to come closer to him. Earlier chapters have indicated just some of the ways in which the church maintains old barriers – and throws up new ones – that make it hard for people to get to Jesus. When I arrived at Hackney I had to get rid of those eight pianos cluttering up our church. Ministry in the inner-city, as elsewhere, is all about house-clearance, the removal of what we can of the debris and detritus that institutionalized religion leaves for people to fall over. By this stage it is hardly necessary to list what must go in the skip.

Clearing out rubbish is a frustrating and unrewarding task. All the more important, then, to rest from time to time on one's broom and to look up, so as to catch sight of where we are going. Despite everything, I enjoyed my time in Hackney. But Hackney is not the home we seek. At my last service in Hackney we sang the hymn, 'Glorious things of thee are spoken, Zion city of our God'. It is a long way from the inner-city to that 'golden city', but Hackney gave me occasional glimpses of it. Those glimpses kept me going.

Before I close this scrapbook of my Hackney years, I leaf through the pages of my diary for a last time. A vignette I had overlooked catches my eye.

People from all the parishes of our 'Episcopal Area' gather for a service of celebration in the church – almost as big as ours – of St Mark's, Dalston. Each parish has been asked to write a prayer. These prayers have been put on cards and tied to helium-filled balloons, one for each parish. At the end of the service we pour out into the churchyard, each parish representative clutching their balloon. At the given signal – '3-2-1 – and lift off!' – the balloons are released so as to sail into the sky, bearing our prayers and praises to the one who rides above the clouds. That, at least, is the intention. In the event the balloons – the cards are too heavy for the helium – hover for a moment, drift briefly in the light breeze, and then sink limply to the ground. There are, no doubt, many morals to be drawn from this misadventure. But I draw none of them, for I am suddenly overwhelmed by a flood of affection for the church I have served so inadequately. As I return to the Rectory I catch myself singing.

References

1 Richard Roberts, *Religion, Theology and the Human Sciences*, Cambridge: Cambridge University Press, 2002.

2 Bernard Walke, *Twenty Years at St Hilary*, London: Methuen, 1935; rev. edn Truro: Truran, 2002.

3 F. W. B. Bullock, *The History of Ridley Hall, Cambridge*, Vol. 1, 1941, Vol. 2, 1953, Cambridge: Cambridge University Press.

4 Michael Botting, *The History of Ridley Hall*, Vol. 3, *Fanning the Flame*, Cambridge: Ridley Hall, 2006.

5 George MacDonald, *Guild Court*, London: Hurst & Blackett, 1868; 1992.

6 Trevor Beeson, *The Bishops*, London: SCM Press, 2003.

7 Albert Schweitzer, *Quest of the Historical Jesus*, Minneapolis: Augsburg Fortress Publishers, 2001.